Write Ideas

ENHAM

An intermediate course in writing skills

WITHDRAWN

Eric Glendinning and Helen Mantell

Longman

Longman Group UK Limited
Longman House, Burnt Mill, Harlow,
Essex CM20 2JE, England
and Associated Companies throughout the world.

First published 1983
Seventh impression 1991

ISBN 0-582-74810-0

Set in Times Roman 10/12 (Linotron 202)
Produced by Longman Singapore Publishers Pte Ltd
Printed in Singapore

Illustrated by: Robin Jacques, G. J. Galsworthy, Oxford Illustrators.

Acknowledgements

We would like to thank H. J. L. Mantell A.R.I.B.A. for his work on the illustrations and all our colleagues at Edinburgh Language Foundation for their help in testing the material.

E. G. and H. M.

We are grateful to the following for permission to reproduce copyright material:

Jonathan Cape Ltd for an extract and four diagrams from *Practical Thinking* by Edward de Bono, illustrated by Alan Tunbridge; Penguin Books Ltd for adapted extracts from pp 204, 197, 431, 262, 412 and 458 *The Penguin Dictionary of Science* by E. B. Uvarov et al (Penguin Reference Books, Fifth Edition 1979) Copyright © Alan Isaacs and E. B. Uvarov 1979.

Longman Group Ltd., for the adaptation of two maps from 'Longman Atlas of Modern British History', 1978 for page 58; for four diagrams from 'Mainline Skills A', 1975 for page 80, and for adapted diagram from 'Nucleus: General Science', 1976 for page 109; Penguin Books Ltd., for a diagram from 'The Penguin Book of the Physical World', 1976, illustrated by David Watson for page 48, 'ROSPA Home Safety' for page 108.

Contents

A Guide to '*Write Ideas*'

Readership
This book is designed for students in the upper years of secondary school or those already in the early stages of tertiary education who require an ability to write English. It is also of value to those preparing for examinations, such as the JMB, which demand a high degree of skill in written English. We assume the reader will have followed a course in general English to intermediate level or above.

Aims and Principles
In our experience, many students find writing the most difficult skill to acquire. Even if they can meet the writing demands made in a general English course, they find difficulty in handling the writing required for study or work. *Write Ideas*, then, aims to equip students to cope with the writing demands made in typical study and work situations.

Good writing involves not only the accurate use of language but also the effective organisation of information. In addition, it requires the writer to be aware of his reader's needs, both when selecting content and guiding the reader through the writing. Another important skill is selecting relevant data to support an argument or explanation. The skills of selecting relevant information, organising it effectively, expressing it in accurate language and guiding the reader through the finished piece of writing are dealt with in this textbook. The writing lesson should not be a totally silent time, with work submitted at the end to the teacher, the sole reader for most student writing, whose response is to return the paper much disfigured with corrections. *Write Ideas* encourages the student to think of his reader as he writes. In many cases, his work will be read and commented on by his fellow students. Students must be given time to think ideas out for themselves and discipline their thoughts on paper; but the exchange of ideas before and comparison of results after writing are an extremely valuable part of the lesson and should not be omitted.

Organisation
This book is divided into eight units. The first three are concerned respectively with techniques of linking facts and ideas, paragraph writing and planning. The remaining five deal with common types of writing, from descriptions of objects and organisations to writing about problems and solutions. The more advanced students may find that they can omit Unit 1, Preparing to Write.

Each unit starts with a 'To make you think' problem and ends with a 'Homework exercises' section. The rest of the unit consists of three to four sections, each more demanding than the previous one. Where required, within sections there are inputs of language and vocabulary (Useful language) and ways to help the reader (Guiding the reader).

Teaching with 'Write Ideas'

The following remarks are intended as a guide to handling different parts of the book.

To make you think

These exercises require the student to complete a brief task or to solve a problem. Most require a short period of individual work, then a comparison in pairs, followed by a class discussion. They are designed to promote discussion of the main points covered in the unit. Using these exercises as a stimulus for thought, students should be able to work out for themselves the basis for organisational points covered in the unit. About 15 minutes is enough to spend on these exercises.

Comment

These brief explanations of key organisational or language points are designed to check that the 'To make you think' exercises have been successful, to provide help for the student using the book on his own and to provide a record of key points for revision and correction purposes. They can be gone through briefly in class and students referred to them when their work is being corrected.

Sections

A section forms a teaching unit and should be completed within two double periods, depending on student level. The first exercise in each section serves a similar purpose to the 'To make you think' exercise but with a narrower focus. It introduces the main teaching point of the section and should be worked through in class. The remaining exercises in each section are progressively more demanding, the final one usually requiring a full-length piece of writing. Wherever possible, students should compare their results in pairs or groups. There are two reasons for this: it leads to a more interesting lesson and, secondly, there are often no 'right answers' in writing. By comparing their writing, students can be helped to reach a deeper understanding of what makes writing effective.

Useful language

These are inputs of structures and vocabulary commonly used in the type of writing being studied. Reference back to these sections can be made by the student tackling later units or by the teacher when correcting students' work.

Guiding the reader
These inputs describe how various 'signposts' can be built into the student's writing to help the reader. Students should be reminded to check they have sufficient guides in the final versions of their work.

Homework exercises
The final section in each unit provides a choice of exercises for students to complete in their own time. The topics are drawn from a range of subject areas to cater for a wide variety of interests. These exercises call for an interest in the subject rather than a specialised knowledge of it. A general interest option is always included. The 'Homework exercises' section should be used when a unit has been completed. When a section has been completed, the final exercise can be set for homework.

Correction
When correcting homework, correction should not be confused with proof-reading. Only major language errors should be corrected and equal effort must be spent on correcting problems of organisation, relevance and reader's guidance. The student can be referred to relevant sections of the book for explanation whenever necessary.

An answer key is not included as many of the exercises are open-ended, and we wish to encourage a variety of response. In addition, we believe that model answers may inhibit rather than guide the student.

1 Preparing to write

To make you think
Study these facts about *James Watt*.

a   He was an engineer.
b   This engineer invented a steam engine.
c   His engine had a special part.
d   The part changed steam back
    into water.
e   Watt was born in Scotland.
f   He made his first
    experiments in Scotland.

Can you link these six facts into three sentences?

Section 1 Linking facts

Look again at sentences (a) and (b). The word *engineer* is in both sentences.
You can join the sentences like this:

   Watt was an engineer *who invented a steam engine.*

The part in italics is a *relative clause.* In the relative clause, you replace *This engineer* by *who. Who* is used for *a person* or *people.*

Look at how you join sentences (c) and (d).

   His engine had a special part *which changed steam into water.*
Which is used for *things.*

Look at how you join sentences (e) and (f).

   Watt was born in Scotland, *where he made his first experiments.*

Where is used for *places* if the place has a preposition (e.g. in, on, at, to,)
before it in the second sentence. If there is no preposition, you use
which.

   Watt was born in Scotland. Scotland is part of Britain.
   Watt was born in Scotland, *which is part of Britain.*

Make sure the relative clause comes immediately after the noun it describes.
What is wrong with this sentence?

   The Nile flows from Lake Victoria, which is the longest river in Africa.

Exercise 1

Choose a personality from the list below. Join the facts together using relative clauses.

1 *Gandhi*

a   Gandhi was a politician.
b   He led the independence movement in India.
c   He studied in London.
d   He became a lawyer in London.
e   He went to South Africa.
f   He became a leader of the Indians in South Africa.
g   He returned to India and helped to lead the nationalist movement.
h   This movement won freedom from Britain in 1947.

2 *Columbus*

a   Columbus was an explorer.
b   He crossed the Atlantic in 1492.
c   He wanted to find a sea-route to Asia.
d   Many valuable things were made in Asia.
e   He discovered a new country.
f   He believed the country was a part of Asia.
g   He called the people Indians.
h   The people lived in the Americas.

3 *Shakespeare*

a   Shakespeare was a writer.
b   He was born in Stratford in 1567.
c   Stratford is a small town.
d   It is in the west of England.
e   Shakespeare wrote many plays.
f   They are still performed today.
g   He spent much of his life in London.
h   He worked in a theatre in London as a writer and actor.

4 *Einstein*

a   Einstein was a great physicist.
b   He was born in Germany in 1879.
c   He developed an important theory.
d   It is called the theory of relativity.
e   He went to live in the USA in 1935 to escape the Nazis.
f   The Nazis took power in Germany.
g   He continued his work in the USA.
h   He died there in 1955.

Exercise 2

Find the relative clauses in these sentences.

1   A biologist is a person who studies living things.
2   Milk which contains chemicals is dangerous.
3   Lhasa, which is in Tibet, is the world's highest capital city.
4   Fleming, who was born in Scotland, discovered penicillin.

Now read the sentences without their relative clauses. How do sentences 1 and 2 differ from 3 and 4 when the clauses are removed?

Comment

Sentence 1 without the relative clause is so general that it tells us almost nothing. Sentence 2 without the relative clause is untrue. These relative clauses contain *essential* information. In contrast, sentences 3 and 4 without their relative clauses are both true and they still contain useful information. The relative clauses contain only *additional* information which is not completely necessary. This type of clause is marked by commas(,).

The first type of clause can be used to make definitions.
Study this diagram.

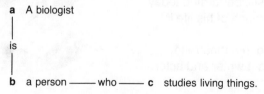

a   A biologist

is

b   a person —— who —— c   studies living things.

You can make a definition of a biologist by joining **a, b** and **c**.

A biologist is a person who studies living things.

Exercise 3

Make 8 definitions using the information in the columns below.

a		b		c
1	a laboratory			has six legs and no backbone
2	a historian			speaks foreign languages well
3	a farm		a person	is concerned with matter and energy
4	an insect		a place	studies the past
5	a linguist		an animal	experiments can be made
6	a library		a science	crops are grown or animals kept
7	a spokesman			books are kept for borrowing
8	physics			speaks for a group

Exercise 4

Write your own definitions of these terms. Compare your definitions with those of another student, then with those in a dictionary.

1   a university
2   a democracy
3   geography
4   a psychologist
5   oxygen

Exercise 5

Rewrite this passage to include the information below it. Use relative clauses. If the information is not essential, mark the clauses with commas.

1   The Olympic Games are an international athletic competition.
2   The name comes from the part of Greece called Olympia.
3   Competitors competed not just in athletics but also in music, poetry and other arts. 4   The modern Olympics concentrate mainly on athletics. 5   The Games open with a ceremony. 6   The Olympic torch is carried by runners. 7   At the end of the ceremony hundreds of doves are released.

a   This international competition takes place every four years.
b   The Games were first held in Olympia over 2000 years ago.
c   Competitors came from all parts of Greece.
d   The modern Olympics were started in 1896.
e   The ceremony is based on the original Greek one.
f   Runners bring the flame from Olympia.
g   Doves are a symbol of peace.

Exercise 6

Study this diagram which describes the United Nations Organisation. Link some of the facts from it to write a short description of the UN. For example:

> The function of the General Assembly, which has over 130 members, is to discuss world problems and to control UN finances.

Find out for yourself other facts about the UN to add to your description. For example, add the name of the Secretary General and of your own country's ambassador.

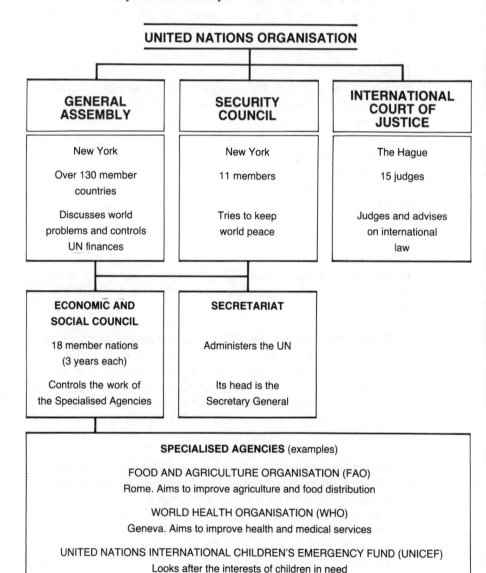

UNITED NATIONS ORGANISATION

GENERAL ASSEMBLY	SECURITY COUNCIL	INTERNATIONAL COURT OF JUSTICE
New York	New York	The Hague
Over 130 member countries	11 members	15 judges
Discusses world problems and controls UN finances	Tries to keep world peace	Judges and advises on international law

ECONOMIC AND SOCIAL COUNCIL	SECRETARIAT
18 member nations (3 years each)	Administers the UN
Controls the work of the Specialised Agencies	Its head is the Secretary General

SPECIALISED AGENCIES (examples)

FOOD AND AGRICULTURE ORGANISATION (FAO)
Rome. Aims to improve agriculture and food distribution

WORLD HEALTH ORGANISATION (WHO)
Geneva. Aims to improve health and medical services

UNITED NATIONS INTERNATIONAL CHILDREN'S EMERGENCY FUND (UNICEF)
Looks after the interests of children in need

Section 2 Linking ideas 1: reason; result

Exercise 7
What is the link between these two sentences? What words can you use to join them?

1   Diamonds are used for drills.
2   Diamonds are very hard.

Look at these two sentences. Which sentence gives a reason? How could you join the sentences?

3   You can see through glass.
4   Glass is used for windows.

Comment
When you write something which your readers may not understand or may not agree with, you can support it with *reasons*. Sentence 2 is a *reason* for sentence 1. To show it is a reason, you can join the sentences in one of these ways:

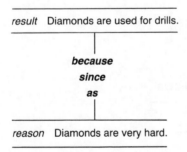

Sentence 4 is a *result* of sentence 3. To show this you can link the sentences using these words:

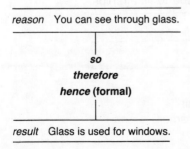

When you use *therefore*, you put a comma or a full stop before it.

You can see through glass, *therefore* it is used for windows.

Note how repeated nouns become pronouns when such sentences are linked.

(Diamonds) are used for drills because (they) are very hard.

You can see through (glass) so (it) is used for windows.

Exercise 8

Choose a suitable statement from the three alternatives given. Then copy and complete the empty boxes. Join the statements in the boxes with a connecting word. Change the repeated nouns to pronouns.

1   *reason*   Wood is cheap and strong.

    result

a   Wood is easy to cut.
b   Wood is used for buildings.
c   Wood burns easily.

2   *reason*   Copper conducts well.

    result

a   Copper is used for electric wires.
b   Copper is a soft metal.
c   Copper is easily made into wires.

3   *result*   Hydrogen was used to fill airships.

    reason

a   Hydrogen is a gas.
b   Hydrogen is lighter than air.
c   Hydrogen has no taste or smell.

4 *reason*   Petrol burns very easily.

result

a Petrol is expensive.
b Petrol is used for cars.
c Petrol must be stored carefully.

5 *result*   Ships are painted.

reason

a Ships carry large cargoes.
b Paint can be of any colour.
c Steel rusts in water.

Exercise 9

Working in pairs, copy the diagrams and complete each blank with
a statement of your own. Then join the two statements with a
connecting word. Compare your answers with those of another
student.

1 We see lightning before we hear thunder.

reason

2 The sun always rises in the east.

reason

3 *reason*

The handles of pots and pans are often made of wood.

4 If we travel in a straight line in any direction, we will eventually return to the point where we started.

_____|_____

reason

_____

5 _result_

_____|_____

The force of gravity on the Moon is much smaller than that on Earth.

Exercise 10

Join each group of facts into one sentence to make a paragraph about desalination plants (places where salt is taken out of sea water). Use relative clauses and any of the connecting words you have studied in this section.

a Sea water cannot be drunk.
b Sea water contains too much salt.
c Sea water has to be desalinated.

d In the Middle East there are many desalination plants.
e In the Middle East there is a shortage of fresh water.
f Desalination plants are factories for changing salt water into drinking water.

g At present these plants use oil.
h Oil is plentiful in the area.

i In the future they may use the power of the sun.
j Solar power is equally plentiful and costs nothing.

Exercise 11

Which nouns do the words in italics refer to? Link each word with the correct noun. The first example is done for you. Mark the book in pencil.

(Honey) is a thick, sweet liquid. (It) is made by bees from the nectar _they_ collect from flowers. _They_ make _it_ because _it_ provides _them_ with food. The bee visits a flower and drinks *its* nectar. *This it* carries home in a honey sac, a kind of bag just in front of *its* stomach. *There* the nectar changes chemically. Water from the nectar must be removed to preserve *it*. *This* is done by evaporation. Finally the bee stores the honey and uses *it* later to feed *its* young.

Section 3 Linking ideas 2: qualification

Study these statements. Both are true. Is there anything that surprises you about them?

1   There is plenty of food in the world.
2   Many people do not have enough to eat.

What words can you use to join these statements? After sentence 1, sentence 2 is unexpected. Sentence 2 is a *qualification*. To show this, you can join the sentences using these words:

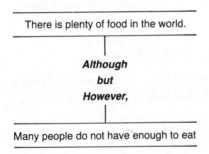

Study how these words are used in these examples:
  a   There is plenty of food in the world *but* many people do not have enough to eat.
  b   There is plenty of food in the world. *However*, many people do not have enough to eat.
  c   *Although* there is plenty of food in the world, many people do not have enough to eat.

Note the punctuation in examples **b** and **c**.

Exercise 12

Link each statement in column **a** with a qualification from column **b**. Remember to change repeated nouns to pronouns.

a	**b**
1 Mars is like the Earth in some ways.	The gold is not easy to recover.
2 The sea contains a lot of gold.	We are not trying hard enough to find new sources of energy.
3 All the oil in the world will soon be used up.	Rice is not grown much.
4 Nuclear power can be used to make electricity.	People can buy less.
5 When there is inflation, people earn more money.	Man cannot live on Mars.
6 Rice can be grown in Europe.	Many people are against using nuclear power.

Guiding the reader   Supporting a qualification

You have now studied three ways of linking ideas. These links help your reader to find his way through your writing and to understand it in the way in which you want him to understand it.

Often when you qualify a statement, the reader expects a reason to support the qualification. For example:

There is plenty of food in the world but many people do not have enough to eat. WHY?

Can you add a reason? One answer is:

There is plenty of food in the world but many people do not have enough to eat *because food supplies are badly distributed*.

Exercise 13

Go back to Exercise 12. Try to add a reason to each sentence you wrote. When you have finished, compare your answers with those of another student.

Exercise 14

Study these different types of cycles and the notes beside each
picture. Then copy and complete the table on page 20.

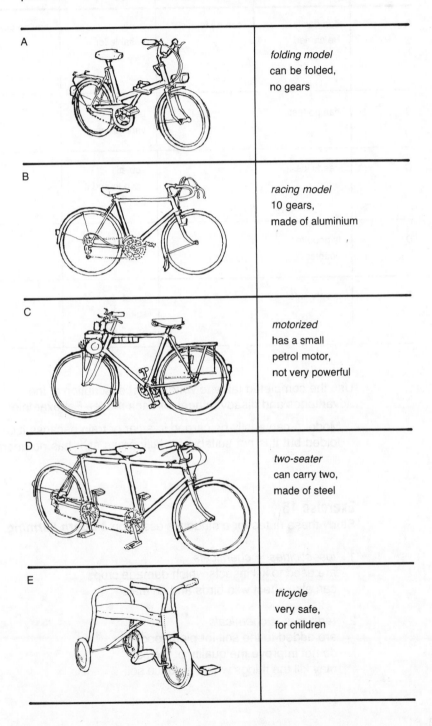

A

folding model
can be folded,
no gears

B

racing model
10 gears,
made of aluminium

C

motorized
has a small
petrol motor,
not very powerful

D

two-seater
can carry two,
made of steel

E

tricycle
very safe,
for children

Model	Advantage	Reason for advantage	Disadvantage	Reason for disadvantage
A	can easily be carried in a car or train	can be folded	is not suitable for hilly areas	has no gears
B	can go fast		is not very strong	
C	needs less effort		you still have to pedal up hills	
D	is good for couples		is heavy	
E	is very safe		is not suitable for adults	

Use the completed table to write a brief description of the advantages and disadvantages of each model. For example:

Model A can easily be carried in a car or train because it can be folded but it is not suitable for hilly areas as it has no gears.

Exercise 15

Study these notes for a student's essay on **Modern Farming**.

1   *insecticides = chemicals*
    are used to kill insects which damage crops
    can also affect wild birds and animals

2   *fertilisers = chemicals*
    are added to the soil for plant food
    do not improve the quality of the soil
    may kill the things which produce soil

3 *steroids = drugs*
   are used to make animals give more meat and less fat
   may affect humans who eat the meat

4 *mechanisation = use of more machines*
   has led to higher outputs
   there are fewer jobs on the land

Use each set of notes to make your own paragraphs about the problems of modern farming. For example:

Insecticides are chemicals which are used to kill insects which damage crops. However, they can also affect wild birds and animals.

Section 4 Homework exercises

Select an exercise from this section which is related to your own field of study or which is of special interest to you. You can complete the exercise in your own time.

For each exercise, join each group of sentences into one sentence. You may omit words and make other changes. Each completed set of sentences should make a paragraph.

1 General Knowledge – Golf
a Golf is a game.
b It was invented in Scotland.
c Golf is still popular in Scotland today.

d You need a set of clubs.

long handle

e

wooden or metal head

f The club is used to hit a small ball round a course.
g The course has 9 or 18 holes.

h In Scotland it is not expensive.
i In many countries it is a rich man's sport.
j Golf courses are private and it costs a lot to use them.

2 *Modern History – Nasser*

a Nasser was an Egyptian
army officer.

b He helped to overthrow the
King of Egypt in 1952.

c The King was corrupt.

d In 1956 Nasser took control
of the Suez Canal.

e The Suez Canal links the
Mediterranean and the Red
Sea.

f Britain and France were
afraid of losing control of the
Canal.

g They invaded Egypt.

h The invasion was a failure.

3 *Medicine – Population trends*

a Far fewer children die in childhood.

b Hygiene and medical treatment have improved.

c This improvement has led to an increased population.

d The birth rate has fallen in Europe.

e The population has doubled in the last 100 years.

f There are far more old people than before.

g The diseases of old age are more important.

2 Paragraph writing

To make you think

These sentences can be reordered to make a paragraph. Put them in the correct order. The first sentence is (c).

a   Only man can talk.
b   Only man has developed the power to destroy himself.
c   Man is the most intelligent of the animals.
d   In many ways man is not superior to animals.
e   Man has made other animals work for him.

Section 1 Meaning links in paragraphs

What makes a good paragraph? A paragraph has meaning links between the sentences in it. You have already studied in Unit 1 some of these links: reason, result and qualification. The meaning structure of the paragraph you have just made is shown below. What connecting words can you add to make the meaning clear to your reader?

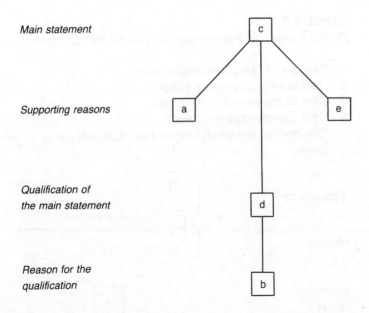

Main statement   c

Supporting reasons   a   e

Qualification of
the main statement   d

Reason for the
qualification   b

Exercise 1

Put these sentences in the correct order to make a paragraph which has the meaning structure shown below. Copy the diagram and write the letter of each sentence in the correct box.

a   More people can read and write.
b   There are more schools but more pupils to fill them.
c   The farmers can grow much more food.
d   It seems that the developing nations have made great progress.
e   There is more food but more mouths to eat it.
f   Real progress is prevented by population growth.

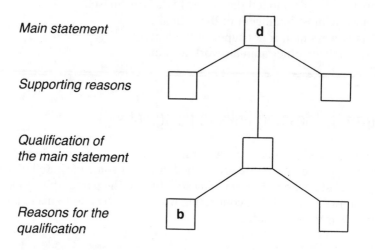

Main statement

Supporting reasons

Qualification of the main statement

Reasons for the qualification

Exercise 2

Do the same with this exercise as you did with Exercise 1.

a   Cars should be prohibited in cities.
b   Cars are destroying our cities.
c   Cars fill the air with poison gas.
d   Cars can damage our health.
e   City centres are being knocked down to make way for new roads.

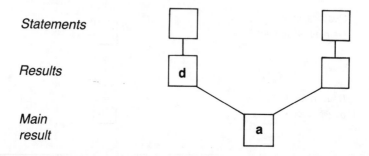

Statements

Results

Main result

Guiding the reader   Missing out connecting words

Connecting words help to make the meaning clear, but are they always necessary? Could any of the connecting words be missed out from this paragraph?

Man is the most intelligent of the animals *because* only he can talk and *because* he has made other animals work for him. *However*, in many ways man is not superior to animals *because* only man has developed the power to destroy himself.

You could miss out the second and third *because*. The meaning link is clear without the connecting word. You could not miss out *however* unless you were certain the reader would understand that the next statement was a qualification.

Go back to Exercises 1 and 2. Write the paragraphs in the correct order. Add connecting words where necessary.

Exercise 3

Study the meaning structure of this paragraph. What kind of statements make up this paragraph? Copy the diagram and label each statement with one of the terms given.

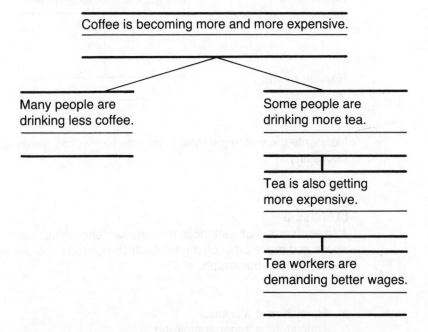

Result 1, Result 2, Main statement, Reason for the qualification, Qualification

What connecting words can you add to make each meaning link clearer? Write the paragraph adding these words where you think they are necessary.

Exercise 4

Copy the diagram and complete the gaps in this paragraph with
statements of your own. The labels indicate the kind of statements
required.

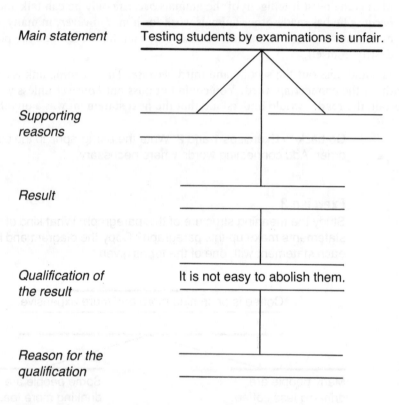

Main statement — Testing students by examinations is unfair.

Supporting reasons

Result

Qualification of the result — It is not easy to abolish them.

Reason for the qualification

Now write the whole paragraph. Include connecting words where
necessary.

Exercise 5

Join each group of sentences into one sentence. You may omit
words and make other changes. Each completed set of sentences
should make a paragraph.

1
a   Agriculture is a science.
b   Agriculture is important to man.
c   Without agriculture we could not feed ourselves.

d   Man may eat some food made from plastics in the future.
e   Food crops like wheat and rice will never be replaced.

f   Some types of meat may disappear.
g   These types of meat require a lot of animal feed to produce.

2
a   Energy cannot be created or destroyed.
b   Energy can be converted into other forms.
c   Energy transformation is never completely efficient.
d   Some energy is changed into unwanted forms.

e   A car engine converts part of the energy into mechanical power.
f   The energy is contained in the fuel.
g   Much of the energy is changed into heat.

Section 2 Grammar links in paragraphs

Exercise 6

There are many links within this paragraph. Some of them have
been made for you. Can you complete the links for the words in
italics? Mark the book in pencil.

1 There is a lot of gold in sea water. 2 Scientists, inventors and
swindlers have tried to make *their* fortune from it. 3 Only the
swindlers, by cheating those who believed *them*, have got rich.
4 *The others* have spent huge sums of money but only tiny
amounts of gold have been recovered. 5 None of the methods
so far developed has been successful. 6 Each process has cost
more to operate than the value of the recovered gold. 7 *The
treasure in the ocean* might just as well not exist.

Comment

A good paragraph has links which help to tie it together. One of the
commonest is that repeated nouns become pronouns. You studied this link in
Unit 1. For example:

gold (sentence 1) becomes *it* (sentence 2)

When there may be misunderstanding or when the repeated noun comes a long
way after it is first mentioned, the full noun is used. Look at this example:

After the *cream* is separated from the *milk, it* is made into butter.

This sentence is confusing because *it* could refer to either *cream* or *milk.*
Therefore you would change *it* to the full noun, *the cream.*

Exercise 7

Rewrite this paragraph. Replace the nouns in italics with pronouns, only if there is no danger that the reader will misunderstand.

1   Newton is one of the fathers of modern science. 2   *Newton's* theory of gravity showed that just as the Earth attracts a falling apple, so *the Earth* attracts the Moon. 3   *Newton* explained that *the Moon* does not fall because *the Moon* is moving round *the Earth*. 4   *The reason* applies also to the planets which are attracted by the Sun. 5   *The planets* do not fall towards *the Sun* because *the planets* are in motion round *the Sun*. 6   Others had tried to explain *the motion of the planets* but none of *the others* had produced as good a theory as *Newton*.

Writers try not to use the same word again and again. They often use an expression which has the same meaning in the context of the paragraph. For example:

   method (sentence 5) becomes *process* (sentence 6)

Exercise 8

Try to improve this paragraph by changing the words in italics to expressions which have the same meaning in the context of the paragraph.

Earthquakes occur somewhere almost every day. Some earthquakes are very slight, but others, like the one which *occurred* in southern Italy in 1980, are very severe. Earthquakes occur in three regions of the Earth. One of the major regions is along the west coast of the Americas. This is also a *region* in which mountain-building has been quite recent. Earthquakes are often caused by movement along an old crack in the rocks deep below the Earth's surface or they may *be caused by* a new crack.

When nouns are first introduced, they have an indefinite article (a, an) or no article if they are plural. When they are mentioned for a second time, the definite article (the) is used. Look back at Exercise 7:

   swindlers (sentence 2) becomes *the swindlers* (sentence 3)

Exercise 9

This paragraph contains examples of all the links mentioned in this section. Show the links by joining the numbered words to other words.

A placebo is a medicine which is given to benefit or to please a patient but not because of its action as a drug. Instead the benefit (1) comes from the psychological effect of taking the drug (2). Often the (3) patient feels better but the improvement may last only a short time. Doctors should therefore prescribe dummy drugs (4) only after other treatment has failed. In addition, the substance (5) should be cheap and harmless unless the patient is paying for it (6) himself. In this case high cost often increases effect.

Section 3 Main ideas in paragraphs

Exercise 10
This passage can be divided into two paragraphs. Where would you divide it?

1   It is easy to see why man made fire a god a long time ago.
2   Fire made it possible for him to live in cold places. 3   It gave him protection from wild animals. 4   With fire he could cook his food and later clear the land to plant crops. 5   In these ways fire made man the most powerful of the animals. 6   Although fire has been part of man's life for many thousands of years, it is only recently that we have been able to explain what fire is. 7   The idea that energy can change from one form to another is not more than 200 years old. 8   Fire is one way in which the chemical energy stored in wood, oil and other fuels is changed into heat energy.

Comment
In Section 1 you saw that in a good paragraph the sentences have meaning links between them. In Section 2 you studied some of the grammar links in a paragraph. The exercise above shows that a good paragraph has one topic. You should have divided the passage at the end of sentence 5 because at that point there is a change of topic. Both paragraphs are about fire but the first one is about why fire was made a god. What is the topic of the second paragraph?

Exercise 11
Identify the topic of each of these paragraphs. Is there one sentence in the paragraph which best summarises the main idea?

1   Wind and water are the causes of soil erosion but both can be controlled by trees. A strong wind can blow away light top soil from an unsheltered field. If trees are planted along the side of the field, they will break the force of the wind. Rain flowing down a hill will cut into the soil and wash it away. Trees slow down the flow of water, absorb much of it and hold the soil together with their roots.

2   Without planning, land would be used for the purpose which would give the biggest profit. No one would think of using land in the centre of cities for parks, schools and hospitals. There would

be nothing to prevent old but beautiful buildings being destroyed to make room for roads and factories. Town planning is essential to balance the needs of the community.

3   In the evening just after sunset we often see a bright object in the west. This is the planet Venus. Although it is our nearest neighbour, no plants or animals like those which live on Earth could exist on Venus. There is no oxygen in the air and the planet is without water. The only rain that falls is acid. The surface of the planet is very hot, at least 475°C.

Guiding the reader   Giving examples

Examples help the reader to understand a difficult point. They also develop general statements. These words can be used to show your reader that you are giving an example:

Rice is grown in humid, tropical countries.

> *for example,*
> *for instance,*
> *to illustrate,*

A lot of rice is cultivated in Indonesia.

Note that it is not always necessary to mark an example in this way.

Exercise 12
Find an example from column (b) to develop each general statement in column (a). Link the statements with a suitable connecting word.

a

1   The stars are very distant from the Earth.

2   Western Europe has large reserves of fuel.

3   Grain crops are grown all over the world.

4   A ship can carry much more than a plane.

5   The population of some Asian countries is increasing rapidly.

6   Animals give us many of our needs.

b

a   A tanker can hold 250,000 tonnes of oil.

b   There are many maize farmers in the USA.

c   The population of Nepal will double in the next 25 years.

d   The brightest star is light years away.

e   Sheep provide us with food and clothing.

f   The UK has a 300 year supply of coal.

Exercise 13
Develop each of these general statements into paragraphs by adding examples of your own.

1   Man is spoiling the Earth by air, water and noise pollution.
2   Many natural materials are used in building.
3   Animals serve us in different ways.

Exercise 14
Write a paragraph to develop each of these topics. Write each sentence on a new line and leave a line between the sentences. Give examples. Include meaning links and grammar links.

1   life on other planets
2   kinds of land transport
3   the value of sport
4   similarities between the work of a doctor and an engineer

When you have completed your paragraph, cut it into strips with one sentence on each strip. Ask another student to put the strips in the correct order. If he cannot, is it his fault or have you not made the meaning links clear enough?

Section 4 Homework exercises

Select an exercise from this section which is related to your own field of study or which is of special interest to you. You can complete the exercise in your own time.

1   *General Knowledge*
    Combine the information which follows into a passage consisting of two paragraphs with the structure indicated below. You will have to order the information first. Suggest a title that will give the main idea of the passage.

Paragraph 1
1   Food builds up the body.
2   Not eating certain foods is important in many religions.
3   Food gives man energy.
4   Food is essential to man.
5   Food is important in other ways.
6   Eating together helps to make the family group stronger.

Paragraph 2
7   The world's population is rising.
8   Scientists are looking for new sources of food.
9   Plankton may also provide food for man.
10 The world's food supplies are not increasing at the same rate.
11 Plankton are tiny sea creatures.
12 People are soon going to have to change their food habits.
13 Oil is a possible new source.

Paragraph 1

Main statement

Supporting reasons

Qualification of the main statement

Reasons for the qualification

Paragraph 2

Statement

Qualification

Result

Examples

Main conclusion

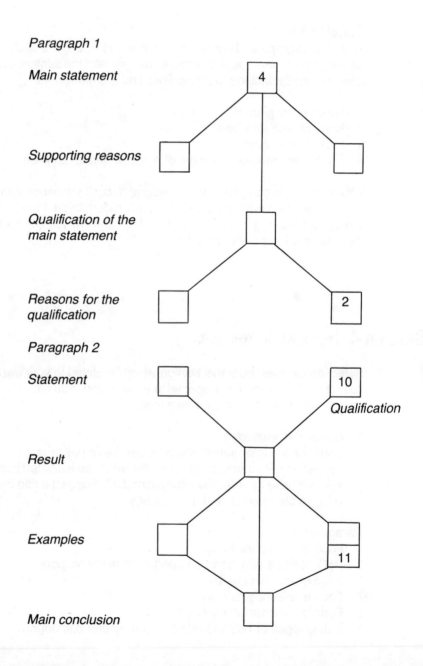

2   *Geography/General knowledge*

Study the map and the notes about Antarctica. Then write a
paragraph including the information on the map and the notes
with the title, *Antarctica, The Coldest Continent*.

Land	permanently covered by very thick ice	
Population	permanent	none
	temporary	hundreds of scientists
Temperature	summer	around 0°C
	winter	−30 to −60°C (the sea freezes)
Wildlife	plants	very few
	birds	many, e.g. penguins
	fish	many kinds
Minerals	copper and lead (but not mined)	

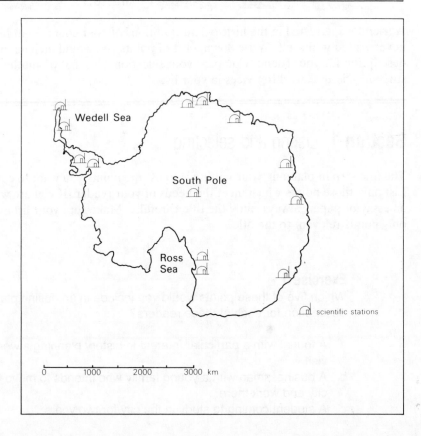

3 Planning your writing

To make you think

A friend is interested in the history and traditions of your country but he has never visited it himself. Write down a list of points you would include in a description for your friend. Compare your selection with that of another student. Discuss any differences in your lists.

Section 1 Listing and selecting

The first step in planning your writing is to list the points you want to cover. List only those points which meet the needs of your reader. If you are writing an essay or paper, always study the title carefully. Make sure your list includes only points relevant to the title.

Exercise 1
Which five of these points would you include in an outline plan of a description for each of these readers?

a   A tourist with a particular interest in history planning a weekend visit.
b   A businessman with a young family who intends to move to the city and work there.
c   A student coming to study in the city for two years.

1 origin and growth
2 industry and commerce
3 places of interest
4 parks
5 shopping areas
6 museums
7 famous people who once lived in the city
8 types of accommodation
9 local government
10 architecture
11 educational facilities
12 restaurants and entertainment
13 sporting facilities
14 city transport

Exercise 2

Which of these points would you include in an answer to this examination question? Tick the points you would choose.

Suggest which form of public transport will be used in cities in the 21st century.

1 advantages and disadvantages of the motor car
2 comparison of road and rail travel
3 tramways
4 advantages of water transport
5 effects of road construction
6 underground railways
7 jet aircraft and pollution
8 bus services
9 animal transport

Compare your list with that of another student. Be prepared to justify your choice.

Exercise 3

List the main points you would include in answers to these questions.

1 Discuss how the high rate of road accidents could be reduced.
2 What are the main problems facing developing countries where oil has just been discovered?
3 What are the advantages and disadvantages of air travel?

Compare your list with that of another student. Then select from both lists the most relevant points.

Section 2 Organising

Exercise 4
Study this list of points from a student's essay on his own country.

1 industry	13 the main regions
2 traditions	14 football teams
3 folk dances	15 economy
4 examinations	16 rivers and lakes
5 geography	17 universities
6 winter sports	18 system of government
7 political parties	19 typical foods
8 education	20 the President
9 farming	21 sport
10 the mountains	22 national dress
11 the national assembly	23 festivals
12 exports	

Try to organise these points into groups. Use some of the points as headings for the groups. For example, 5 *geography* can be a heading for a group which includes 10 *the mountains*.

Having listed and selected your points, you must *organise* your material. You can start by grouping your material under headings as you did above. Each of these groups can later be expanded into a paragraph or section of your writing.

Next, decide on the order of your groups. You can organise histories and processes in order of time. Descriptions of places or things may be organised in order of the importance of their parts, or in the order in which their parts appear to lie; for example, most important to least important, top to bottom, left to right or outside to inside.

Remember the first three stages of planning your writing should always be:

list   select   organise

Exercise 5
Organise these points for an essay on **Tigers** into suitable groups. Give each group a heading.

1 method of killing prey	7 2000 in India
2 length	8 breeding
3 the Bengal tiger	9 speed
4 prey	10 time of hunting for prey
5 weight	11 150 in Nepal
6 the Siberian tiger	12 colour

Exercise 6

Organise these points for an essay on *Health Care* into suitable groups. Give each group a heading.

1 smallpox vaccination introduced
2 overcrowded houses
3 local medical officers appointed
4 more money spent on health services
5 poor food
6 cancer
7 antiseptics introduced into surgery
8 more doctors
9 poor water supply
10 anaesthetics first used
11 heart disease
12 more hospital beds
13 training for nurses
14 free medical care for all

Exercise 7

Organise this material for an essay on the *History of Flying*. Compare your order with that of another student.

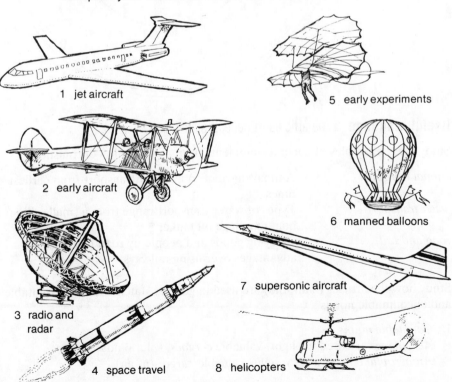

1 jet aircraft

5 early experiments

2 early aircraft

6 manned balloons

3 radio and radar

7 supersonic aircraft

4 space travel

8 helicopters

Exercise 8

List the points you would include in a paragraph describing the composition of the Earth. Use the diagram to help you. Compare your answer with that of another student. Then write the paragraph.

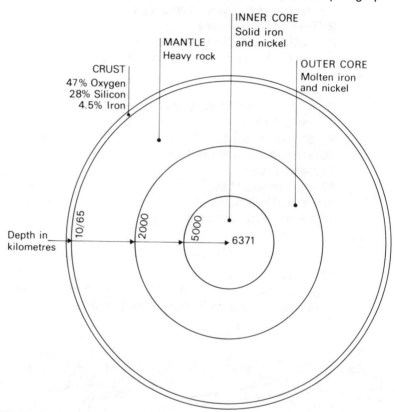

Useful language   The articles in general statements

Study these examples of general statements from a description of transport.

animal transport   Animals have been used for transport from earliest times.

water transport   Types of water transport range from a small sailing boat to a huge oil tanker.

road and rail   Carrying goods and people by road has many advantages over using railways.

Study how the articles (a/an, the) are used in general statements with countable and uncountable nouns.

1   *Countable nouns*
    Aeroplanes are used for light, valuable *cargoes.* (plural nouns) or
    An aeroplane is used for *a* light, valuable *cargo.* (a, an)

2　*Uncountable nouns*
Cheap *transport* is necessary before *industry* can develop. (no article)

Compare these specific statements:
The first aeroplane to cross the Atlantic was a biplane.
The cheapest transport for *the* iron industry in Britain was canals.

Exercise 9

Study this list of headings for an essay on **Agriculture**. Then expand each into a general statement. You need not use the exact words of the headings.

1　the importance of agriculture
2　food crops
3　industrial crops
4　animals
5　problems faced by farmers
6　farming in the future

Section 3 Supporting and presenting

Exercise 10

Here are three general statements from an essay on **Agriculture**.

a　*food crops*
　　Food crops can be divided into grains, fruits and beverages.
b　*the importance of agriculture*
　　As the world's population increases, agriculture grows more important.
c　*problems faced by farmers*
　　Farmers have to face problems caused by the weather, by pests and by diseases.

Study the statements which follow. Which of them would you use to support the general statements above? Write a, b or c against the relevant supporting statements. Some of the data is *not* relevant.

1　Rice is the major food crop in most of Asia.
2　There will be 8000 million mouths to feed by the end of the century.
3　Collective farms are found in the USSR.
4　Rats eat one fifth of the world's rice.
5　Cotton is an important industrial crop.

6   Coffee and tea provide employment for many in East Africa and in India.
7   The nations which produce food will be the leading countries of the future.
8   Heavy rain can destroy crops.
9   Cattle are kept for milk and meat in the USA.
10 Oranges are a Mediterranean crop.

Comment

In Exercise 10 you chose supporting data to expand three general statements. In the same way that your headings must be relevant to your reader's needs, so your supporting statements must be relevant to the general statements. Statements 3 and 9 in Exercise 10 are not relevant to any of the three general statements.

Exercise 11

Select relevant information from this list to support each of these general statements. Not all of the data given is relevant. Make a chart yourself and tick the appropriate column.

a   *Before the invention of coins, many different things were used for money.*
b   *Money has three uses: it can be used as a medium of exchange, a measurement of value, a way of planning for the future.*

	a	b
1 Money allows us to compare quite different things, such as a visit to the cinema and a loaf of bread.		
2 In North Africa people were paid in salt.		
3 Exchanging goods is called barter.		
4 Money allows governments to make budgets.		
5 The Chinese invented coins and paper money.		
6 Small shells were used as money in parts of India.		
7 Iron was the medium of exchange in West Africa.		
8 Money saves us the trouble of bartering for the hundreds of things we need every day.		
9 The most valuable coins were made of gold and silver.		

Compare your answer with that of another student. Then develop each general statement, a and b, into a paragraph using the data you have selected. You may add extra examples of your own to make a good paragraph.

Guiding the reader   Listing sentences; Definitions and examples

The final stage in writing is to check that the reader can easily find his way through your writing. Here are two more ways to guide the reader:

1   *Listing sentences*
Listing sentences help the reader to know what the order of points will be. Study these examples of listing sentences.

1   There are three kinds of food crops: grains, fruits and beverages.
2   We can group food crops into grains, fruits and beverages.
3   Food crops can be divided into grains, fruits and beverages.

The sentences or paragraphs which follow a listing sentence deal with the points in the order in which they are listed. For example:

Farmers have to face problems caused by the weather, by pests and by diseases. Too much rain and the crops never ripen, too little and they die. Pests eat or spoil their crops. Diseases kill their animals and crops.

2   *Definitions and examples*
Definitions (see Unit 1) and examples (see Unit 2) can be added to help the reader understand any unfamiliar terms. For example, you could make the last sentence in the paragraph above clearer by adding:

Diseases kill their animals and crops. *Rust, for instance, is a disease which attacks wheat.*

Exercise 12
Study this information. Combine the information into a paragraph on **Food Crops**. Add any information of your own or use a dictionary to help you.

a   *grains*:   wheat, rice, barley, rye etc.
    fruits: apples, apricots, figs etc.
    beverages: tea, coffee, cocoa etc.

b   *Areas where cultivated*:
    grains: all parts of the world
    fruits: all parts of the world
    beverages: tropical and some sub-tropical areas (Asia, Africa and South America)

c *Areas where consumed:*
   grains: all countries of the world
                    (basic diet of the world's population)
   fruits: mainly Europe and North America
   beverages: all countries of the world
                    (Britain imports one-third of all tea grown)

Exercise 13

Study the information below. Combine these facts and any information
of your own to write a paragraph about **The Solar System**.

the sun   a dense sphere of glowing matter
planets   nine bodies of matter
                 (revolve in orbits round the sun; the smallest –
                 Mercury; the largest – Jupiter)
asteroids   large pieces of rock
                 (revolve between Mars and Jupiter)
meteors   pieces of stone and iron
                 (enter the atmosphere, glow and evaporate)
other bodies   comets (clouds of gas and ice with a bright head)
                 dust
                 gases

Section 4 Homework exercises

Select an exercise from this section which is related to your own
field of study or which is of special interest to you. You should
complete the exercise in your own time.

1 *General knowledge*

a Study the map of San Riposta and the other data given. Select
   and list the points you would include in a description of the
   city for an encyclopaedia entry. Group them under headings
   such as:

   cultural interest
   industry and commerce

b Expand your points into general statements and add any
   relevant supporting information from the data given to write a
   publicity leaflet marking the anniversary of the founding of the
   city. Add any guidance you feel necessary for your reader and
   check your paragraph divisions.

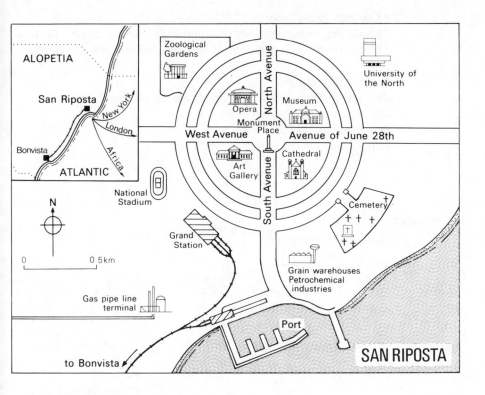

Development

1801	first settlers
1830	port opened
1850–60	centre built by a French engineer
1861	opera opened
1871	June 28th. City liberated by General Vesta
1901	monument erected
1911	railway constructed
1968	gas pipeline terminal built
1975	petrochemical industry started

Other facts

population	120,000
industries	petrochemicals
	agricultural machinery
	port
newspapers	Daily Herald
	Evening Star

2   *General knowledge*

Study this information about World War 1 fighter planes. Some of the information is given in notes and some in the diagrams.

Early fighter planes
- very few instruments, only a compass (for direction) and an altimeter (for height), no radio
- no protection for the crew
- fragile body (wood, wire and cloth)

a   **Vickers EFB5, 1915**

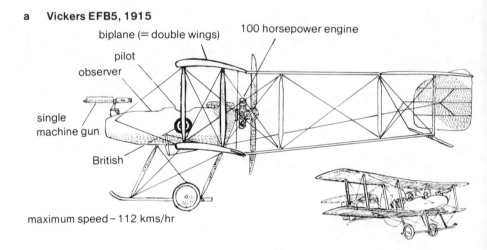

biplane (= double wings)   100 horsepower engine
pilot
observer
single machine gun
British

maximum speed – 112 kms/hr

b   **Fokker Monoplane E3, 1915**

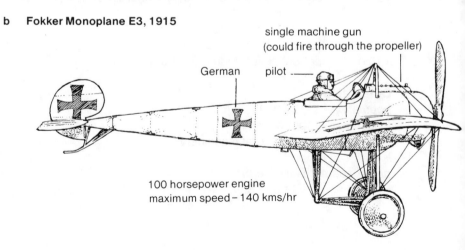

single machine gun
(could fire through the propeller)
German   pilot
100 horsepower engine
maximum speed – 140 kms/hr

c   **Spad 13, 1917**

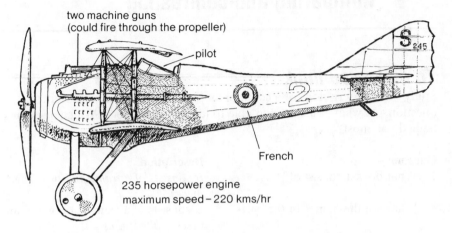

two machine guns
(could fire through the propeller)

pilot

French

235 horsepower engine
maximum speed – 220 kms/hr

Combine the information into paragraphs; an introductory
paragraph using the information in the notes, followed by a
paragraph on each plane. Each paragraph on the planes should
present the information in this order:

1 type
2 date and nationality
3 crew
4 arms
5 engine details and speed

4 Describing objects and organisations Comparing and contrasting

To make you think

Study these descriptions of a common object. Each answer a different question. At what point are you able to identify the object? Which questions helped you most?

Question	Description
1 What does it consist of?	*It consists of a frame and two other pieces.*
2 What are the names of the parts?	It consists of a frame and two other pieces *called skins.*
3 What shape is it?	It consists of a *cylindrical* frame and two *circular* pieces called skins.
4 What is it made of?	It consists of a cylindrical *wooden* frame and two circular *plastic* skins.
5 How are the parts connected?	It consists of a cylindrical wooden frame and two circular plastic skins, *one fitted over each end.*
6 What is it used for?	It consists of a cylindrical wooden frame and two circular plastic skins, one fitted over each end. *It is used as a musical instrument.*
7 How is it used?	It consists of a cylindrical wooden frame and two circular plastic skins, one fitted over each end. It is used as a musical instrument. *The musician beats the skins with his hands or with special sticks.*

Section 1 Planning a description

When you describe something you should try to think of the kind of questions your reader would want to ask about the object. Your plan can consist of an ordered list of reader's questions. Some possible questions are listed above. Others which might be useful for a description are:

What colour is it?
What are its dimensions?
What special characteristic has it?

Try to add other questions to this list.

Exercise 1
Look at this drawing of a *mhor*.

What questions does the drawing answer for you? What additional questions might you ask? How would you order the questions? Compare your list with that of another student.

Exercise 2
Your partner will think of an object. Ask your partner questions until you can identify the object. Write down the questions which helped you most.

Repeat the exercise for several different objects. Then compare your list with your partner's list. Are your questions like those on page 46?

Exercise 3
Study this description of an optical microscope.

A microscope is an instrument which is used by scientists to magnify very small objects to make them visible. The commonest type is the optical microscope. An optical microscope consists of a lens tube, a slide platform, an object condenser and a metal frame.
5 The lens tube contains a number of lenses, the most important of which are the ocular and objective lenses. The lenses are for magnifying the object. The slide platform contains a number of clamps for holding the slides. The object condenser is composed of a lens and a diaphragm. The latter is used to control the amount of
10 light entering the lens tube. The frame is made up of two parts: a heavy base and a swivelling top. The optical microscope is good enough for ordinary laboratory work but for research the much more powerful electron microscope is used.

How many of the questions on page 46 can be answered from this description? In what order are they answered? Is this the best order?

Exercise 4

Study this picture of a microscope. What information is more clearly presented in the picture than in the text? Could the text be changed to give more of the information in the picture?

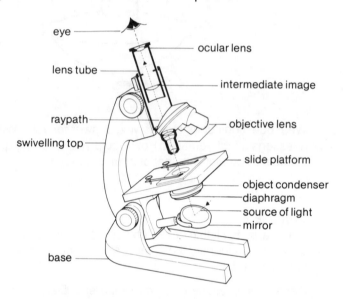

Useful language Consist of, comprise, etc.

To answer the question *What does it consist of?*, we use a small group of verbs:

We can answer the question *What is it used for?* like this:

1   A drum is *used to make* music.
2   A drum is *used for making* music.
3   A drum is *used as* a musical instrument.
4   We can make music *using/with* a drum.

Exercise 5

Study these objects. List as many possible uses as you can for
each one. When you have finished, compare your list with that of
another student. For example:

> *A brick* can be used for building.
> as a weapon.
> to hold a door open.

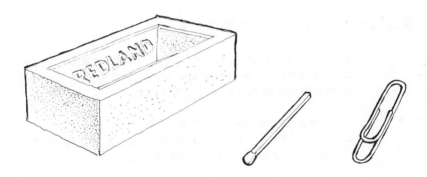

Exercise 6

Copy and complete this diagram which breaks down an optical
microscope like the one on page 48 into its components, using the
information given in Exercise 3.

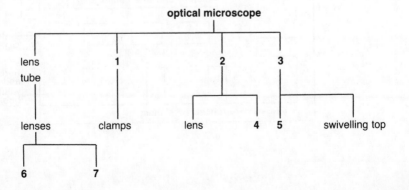

Now write a short paragraph describing what a microscope consists of. Use the completed diagram and the picture of the microscope to help you. Do not look back at the text until you have completed your paragraph. Then compare your description with the text.

Exercise 7

Write a description of an object which is well known to you but is not well known to your classmates. For example, you can describe a traditional cooking pot, musical instrument or boat used in your country. You may add a drawing to complete your description.

When you have written your description, exchange it with that of another student. Read his description carefully. Then add to it any questions about the object which you feel are still unanswered.

Section 2 Homework exercises

Select an exercise from this section which is related to your own field of study or which is of special interest to you. You can complete the exercise in your own time.

1 *General knowledge – A library*
a   Look at this diagram of a library and the description opposite. Why is the description a bad description?

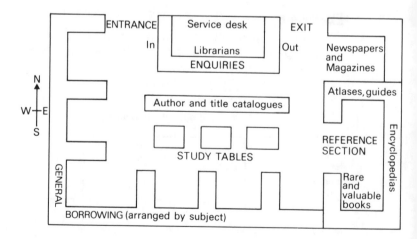

Details of all books can be found in the catalogues. The Reference section contains encylopaedias, atlases and rare or valuable books. When you enter the library, the service desk is on your left. Books for general borrowing are on your right and on the wall facing you. Reference books cannot be borrowed. The Service Desk deals with any enquiries, for example, about reserving books. The catalogues are arranged according to author and title. The books for general borrowing are shelved according to subject. The newspapers and magazines are for reading in the library only. The librarian will also give advice on where to find books on any subject. A selection of newspapers and magazines is kept near the Exit. Books are returned and stamped for borrowing at the Service Desk.

b Prepare a plan for your own description of the library. Then write your description.

2 Science – Cell structure

a Read this description of a cell.
All living things are made up of many units which are called cells. Each cell contains a nucleus which is surrounded by a jelly-like substance known as the cytoplasm. The cytoplasm contains various organelles concerned with important tasks such as generating energy. The outside of the cell is a membrane which controls the cell's intake and output.
The nucleus is the most important part of the cell. It controls the main functions of the cell. It is filled with a special type of cytoplasm called nucleoplasm.

b Copy the diagram and fill in the labels with the words below.

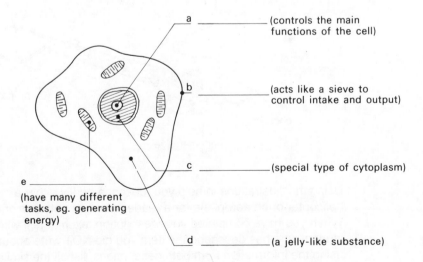

a _____ (controls the main functions of the cell)

b _____ (acts like a sieve to control intake and output)

c _____ (special type of cytoplasm)

d _____ (a jelly-like substance)

e _____
(have many different tasks, eg. generating energy)

cytoplasm, nucleus, organelles, membrane, nucleoplasm

c   Decide on the best order for describing the different parts of the cell. Then write your own description of a cell using only the notes and the diagram without referring to the text. Start your description with a listing sentence (See Unit 3).

Section 3 Comparing and contrasting

Exercise 8

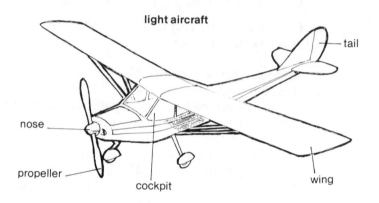

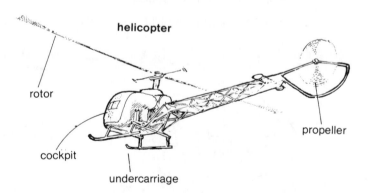

Using the illustrations to help you, describe briefly either a helicopter or an aeroplane for a reader who has not seen one. When you have completed your description, exchange it with a student who has described the item you did NOT write about. Then, using the information from both descriptions, list all the similarities and differences you can find between these two forms of air transport.

Comment

A description often compares and contrasts objects, ideas, organisations, etc.
This kind of description is often used:

1   when the reader knows one of the items described but not the other.
2   when the writer is assessing the value of different proposals, solutions and
    explanations. (See Units 6 and 8)
You can show contrasts and similarities on a chart, like this:

Feature	Helicopter	Aeroplane
propellers	rotor and tail	nose
wings	none	two
flight	all directions	forward only
take-off	vertical, no runway	runway needed

What other features for comparison and contrast can you add to this chart?

Exercise 9

Prepare a chart for comparing and contrasting a cycle and a
motorcycle. List the key features for comparison and contrast.
Decide how the features should be grouped and how the groups of
features should be ordered. For example, you might put *controls*
and *parts* in one group, *speed* and *size* in another.

Compare your list of features with another student's list. Discuss
the lists and try to agree on the best way of arranging the features.
Then work together to fill in the details for each item. Use an
illustrated dictionary to help you if necessary.

Useful language   Describing differences and similarities

We can describe differences using:

1   The comparative form of the adjective or adverb. For example:
    Aeroplanes can fly *faster than* helicopters.
    Helicopters are *more manoeuvrable than* aeroplanes.

2 The connecting words, *but, whereas, in contrast.* For example:
> An aeroplane has wings *whereas* a helicopter has not.
> An aeroplane has wings. *In contrast* a helicopter has not.

3 *unlike, different from* For example:
> *Unlike* the aeroplane, the helicopter does not require a runway.
> The helicopter *is different from* the aeroplane in that the propeller is above the body.

We can describe similarities using these expressions:

4 *as . . . as* For example:
> Helicopters are *as* expensive *as* aeroplanes.

5 *both . . . and* For example:
> *Both* helicopters *and* aeroplanes are used for air transport.

6 *neither . . . nor* For example:
> *Neither* the helicopter *nor* the aeroplane requires any kind of track.

Exercise 10

Study these entries from a dictionary of science. Note the meaning of these abbreviations.
A.W. atomic weight   At.No. atomic number   m.p. melting point   b.p. boiling point   S.G. specific gravity

Hydrogen   H. Element. A.W. 1.00797. At. No. 1. A colourless, odourless, tasteless gas. The lightest substance known. It is inflammable and combines with oxygen to form water. Occurs in water, in organic compounds and in all living things.

Helium   He. Element. A.W. 4.0026. At. No. 2. An inert gas which occurs in certain natural gases in the USA, in radioactive ores, and in the atmosphere. Non-inflammable, very light, valuable for filling airships and balloons.

Tin   Sn. Element. A.W. 118.69 At. No. 50. A silvery-white metal, S.G. 7.31, m.p. 231.85°C, which is soft, malleable and ductile. The metal is extracted by heating the oxide with powdered carbon. Used for tin-plating and in many alloys.

Mercury   Hg. Element. A.W. 200.59. At. No. 30. A liquid, silvery-white metal, S.G. 13.6, m.p. -39°C, b.p. 357°C. Extracted by roasting the ore in a current of air. Used in thermometers. Alloys used in dentistry. Compounds are poisonous; some are used in medicine.

Sulphuric Acid   A colourless, oily acid. S.G. 1.84. Extremely corrosive, reacts violently with water. Used extensively in many processes in the chemical industry and in the lead accumulator.

Water   The normal oxide of hydrogen. Pure water is a colourless, odourless liquid, m.p. 0°C, b.p. 100°C, which has a maximum density of 1.00 gramme per c.c. at 4°C.

Now write a sentence of comparison or contrast for each point listed in the table below.

Point of comparison/contrast	Entries
1 type of element	helium, tin
2 colour	mercury, tin
3 colour, odour	hydrogen, water
4 properties	hydrogen, helium
5 method of extraction	tin, mercury
6 specific gravity	sulphuric acid, mercury
7 uses	mercury, tin
8 type of element	sulphuric acid, water

Useful language   Marginally, rather, twice as, etc.

Look at this table of population figures for some UK cities.

Belfast	335,000
Cardiff	278,221
Edinburgh	453,584
Glasgow	897,483
London	7,379, 014

You can compare the population sizes using the methods given on page 54. For example:

1   London is *larger than* Edinburgh.

But a statement like this gives no indication of the degree of difference between the cities. To show this you can use the following expressions:

2   Edinburgh is *marginally/slightly* bigger than Belfast.
3   Edinburgh is *rather/considerably* bigger than Cardiff.
4   London is *much/substantially* bigger than Edinburgh.

To indicate a difference of a certain amount, we can say:

5   Glasgow is *twice* as big as Edinburgh.
6   Glasgow is *three times* as big as Cardiff.

Exercise 11

Compare the population sizes of these cities:

Brussels	1,075,000
Cairo	8,145,000
Djakarta	6,000,000
Dacca	2,000,000
Bogota	5,000,000
Tripoli	837,000
La Paz	1,140,000
Peking	8,700,000

Guiding the reader   Opening sentences

To help your reader, the opening sentence of your writing, or the opening paragraph in a longer piece of writing, should introduce the main topic. There is no special form for an opening sentence. Study these examples of opening sentences for texts of comparison and contrast:

The Earth differs from other planets in terms of its size, atmosphere, and the time it takes to travel round the Sun.

There are many similarities between the work of an engineer and a doctor.

What opening sentence can you suggest for a comparison and contrast of a helicopter and an aeroplane?

Exercise 12

Study this passage.

The domestic hen has short wings which it rarely uses because it has a heavy body and lives on the ground. It is clumsy in flight and can cover only short distances. Its feet are designed for scratching the ground to find seeds and worms. It has a short beak adapted for
5 eating this kind of food although it will also eat almost any other kind of food. Hens nest on the ground. They have been bred for egg production and can lay up to 300 eggs a year.
Hawks have long, pointed, powerful wings for high, rapid flight.
10 Their feet are designed to catch and grasp small birds and other small animals. Their beaks are sharp, for cutting up the animals they kill. They nest in trees and on high places. Hawks lay 3 to 6 eggs at a time and may lay twice a year.
A duck has webbed feet so that it can swim easily and walk on soft
15 ground. It has a long, flat beak which it uses to search for food in river and pond mud. It has powerful wings which enable it to fly long distances. It nests in grass at the water's edge. Ducks migrate long distances. A duck lays 5 to 12 eggs at a time and may lay twice a year.

Copy the chart and use the information in the passage to complete it.

Feature	Hen	Hawk	Duck
eggs			
wings			
feet			
beak			
flight			
nest			
migration			
food			

Exercise 13

Divide the features in the left-hand column into three related groups. Some features have been filled in for you.

> *group 1*   feet, _____, food
> *group 2*   _____, _____
> *group 3*   _____, wings, _____

Now write a comparison and contrast of the three birds. Organise your writing so that each paragraph covers one group of features. Your writing should have this organisation:

> paragraph 1   group 1
> paragraph 2   group 2
> paragraph 3   group 3

You will also need to write an opening sentence to introduce your reader to the topic.

Exercise 14

Prepare a chart for comparing and contrasting your country with any one of its neighbours. Your chart should list the key features to be compared and contrasted. Fill in the chart. Then write a passage of comparison and contrast.

Now write a comparison and contrast of the two countries. Remember to group related features into paragraphs and begin with a suitable opening sentence. Exchange your completed essay with that of another student. Ask him to prepare a chart based on the information in your essay. Then compare your original chart with his.

Section 4 Homework exercises

Select an exercise from this section which is related to your own field of study or which is of special interest to you. You can complete the exercise in your own time.

1 *History – Old and new Edinburgh*
   Study these two maps of Edinburgh, one of the town before 1770 and the other in 1820, after it had expanded greatly. Using these and the accompanying notes, write an essay comparing and contrasting Edinburgh at the two dates.

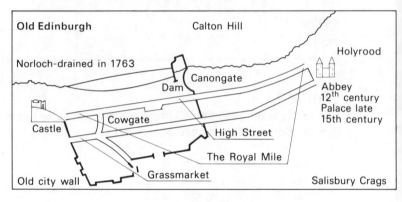

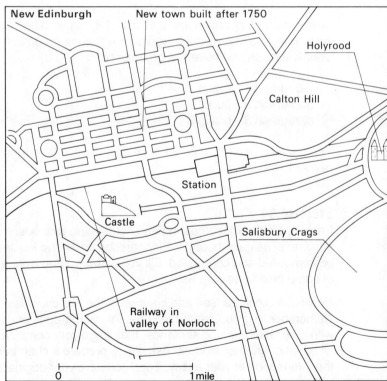

	before 1770	**1820**
population:	48,000	150,000
housing:	tall, narrow buildings many families crowded in each house	large, spacious buildings fewer people per house
streets:	dirty, narrow, twisting no green spaces	squares, parallel streets curving streets many parks and gardens
industries and commerce:	paper-making, beer-making, banking	beer-making, banking, insurance, printing

2   *Geography – The climate of the Zambesi region and of Toronto*

a   Study these climatic details for Toronto, Canada and the Zambesi Region of Central Africa on page 60.

b   Write a short comparison and contrast of the climates of the two areas.

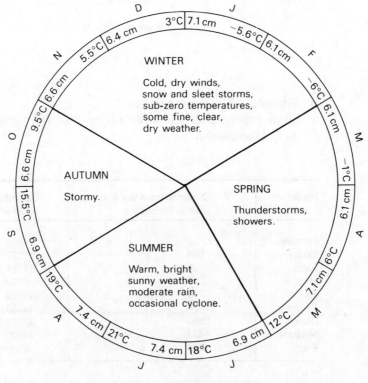

TORONTO

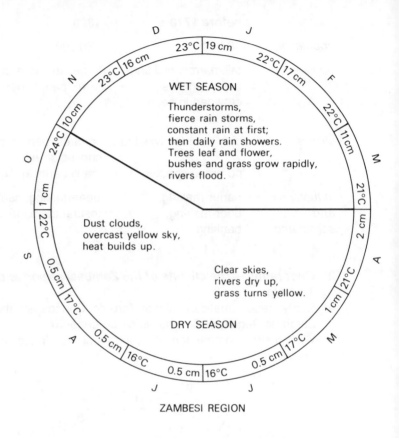

ZAMBESI REGION

3   *Science – The Solar System*

a   Study these tables, then write a comparison and contrast of any four of the planets.

Planet	Distance from the Sun (*million kilometres*)	Diameter (*kilometres*)
Mercury	58	4840
Venus	108	12228
Earth	150	12751
Mars	228	6742
Jupiter	779	140720
Saturn	1426	116820
Uranus	2850	47100
Neptune	4493	44600
Pluto	5898	5500

Planet	Satellites	Revolution round the Sun	Maximum surface temp °C	Atmosphere
Mercury	0	88 days	395	none
Venus	0	225 days	475	some water vapour a lot of carbon dioxide
Earth	1	365 days	60	nitrogen, oxygen, carbon dioxide, water vapour
Mars	2	687 days	24	no oxygen, little water vapour
Jupiter	13	12 years	−93	hydrogen, methane, ammonia
Saturn	10	30 years	−115	compressed methane, ammonia
Uranus	5	84 years	−155	mainly hydrogen, some methane
Neptune	2	165 years	−183	mainly hydrogen, some methane
Pluto	0	248 years	?	?

5 Describing processes, developments and graphs

To make you think

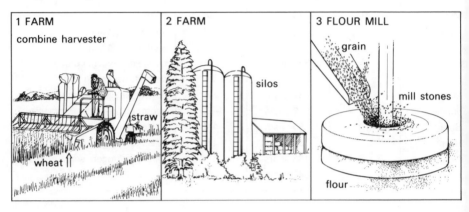

Put these events in the process of bread-making in order.

a   The grain is made into flour.
b   The loaves are sold.
c   The flour is mixed with other ingredients.
d   The grain is stored.
e   The wheat is harvested.
f   The mixture is baked into loaves.

Section 1 Describing processes

The first step in planning a description of a process is to list the main events in order.

Guiding the reader   Marking sequence

You can mark the order of events with sequence words:

First/To begin with
Then/Next/Afterwards/Later
Finally

You can also use time clauses with *after* and *before* to show sequence. For example:

Action 1   The grain is stored.
Action 2   The grain is made into flour.

After the grain is stored, it is made into flour.

Before the grain is made into flour, it is stored.

The Present Perfect tense is used to make absolutely clear that one event happened before another. For example:

After the wheat *has been harvested*, the grain is stored.

The Past Perfect is used for the same purpose when describing a process which occurred in the past. For example:

After the wheat *had been harvested*, the grain was stored.

Exercise 1
Go back to the *To make you think* activity. Write out the list of events. Show the correct order using any of the different methods described above. (Information is required from the illustration as well as the boxes – i.e. from the whole diagram.)

The next step is to add any important supplementary information. The information you give will depend on who your reader is.

What other information would your reader need to know about the bread-making process? The diagram below shows some of the information that could be added.

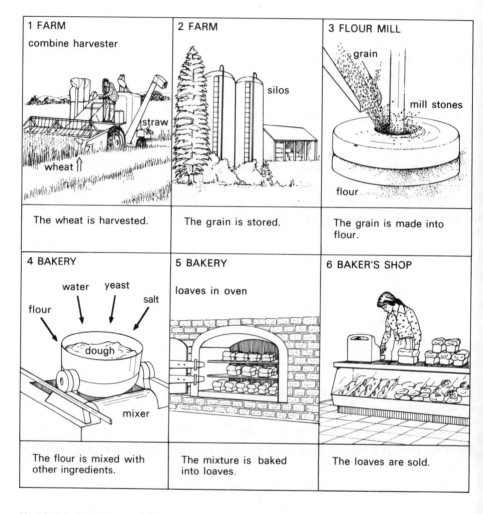

1 FARM	2 FARM	3 FLOUR MILL
combine harvester	silos	grain / mill stones
straw / wheat		flour
The wheat is harvested.	The grain is stored.	The grain is made into flour.

4 BAKERY	5 BAKERY	6 BAKER'S SHOP
water yeast salt / flour / dough / mixer	loaves in oven	
The flour is mixed with other ingredients.	The mixture is baked into loaves.	The loaves are sold.

Useful language   Adding information on place, purpose and method

You studied in Unit 1 how information can be added to a sentence using relative clauses. Note these methods of adding information on place, method and purpose.

Place
The grain is stored *in a silo.*
The grain is made into flour *at a flour mill.*
The loaves are taken to a baker's shop, *where they are sold.*

Method
The dough is made to rise *by* add*ing* yeast.

Purpose
Yeast is added *so that* the dough will rise.
Yeast is added *to make* the dough rise.
Yeast is added *because* it makes the dough rise.

Exercise 2

To your list of events in the bread-making process, add as much of the information contained in the diagram as you can.

Exercise 3

Use this plan to describe the process of planning and building a new road. Your reader is not an engineer. Use any of the extra information given below each event, or any information of your own that you think necessary.

1 **The needs are assessed.**	2 **The route is planned.**	3 **Soil samples are taken.**
The number of vehicles using roads in the area are counted.	Hills, small towns and rivers are avoided where possible. Bridges are very expensive.	Holes are bored into the soil and rock. The strength and wetness of the soil is measured.
4 **The route is cleared and levelled.**	5 **Thick layers of concrete are put down.**	6 **The top surface is laid and traffic guides are added.**
Large bulldozers and scrapers are used.	A paver is used to spread the concrete evenly. The concrete makes a good foundation.	Normally the top surface is tarmac. Cat's eyes are put in. They guide the driver at night.

Guiding the reader   Paragraphing

Dividing your writing into paragraphs is a way of controlling the amount of information you give to your reader at one time. In descriptions of processes, paragraph divisions usually coincide with the main stages of a process. However, if the units of information are quite short, you can include several stages in one paragraph. Remember that a paragraph division should not cut through stages.

In a description of bread-making, a possible division would be:

Paragraph 1	The wheat is harvested.
	The grain is stored.
	The grain is made into flour.
Paragraph 2	The flour is mixed with other ingredients.
	The mixture is baked into loaves.
	The loaves are sold.

Where would you divide your description of road building?

Section 2 Describing developments

Exercise 4
Study this time scale. It shows the stages in the development of an imaginary African city.

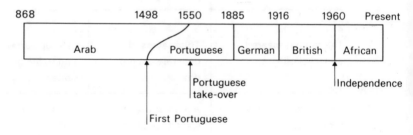

How would you organise the following pieces of information for a history of the city?

a   Arabic was the most important language.
b   The German Emperor visited the city.
c   English was taught in all the schools.
d   Independence Park was opened.
e   A fort was built to give protection against the Arabs.
f   The city was founded.
g   The Germans were defeated.
h   The city was shelled by the British Navy.
i   The city traded with all parts of the Arab empire.

Comment

The best way to organise material like this is, first, to group the material according to main stages and, then, to order it within the stages. In this example, the material can first be grouped according to the occupying powers – Arabs, Portuguese, etc. Within each of these groups, you can then order it from the earliest event to the most recent. Some of the events, such as (a) and (i) refer to whole periods.

Guiding the reader   Ways of showing time relationships

1   You can show the time of an event in a sequence by using time prepositions. For example:

a   *During* the German period, German was taught in all schools.
b   *In* the ninth century, the city was founded.
c   *After* 1916, the British controlled the city.

2   You can also use time clauses. For example:

a   To show actions in close succession: *when*

Action 1   The British attacked the city.
Action 2   The Germans were driven out.

When the British attacked the city, the Germans were driven out.

b   To show simultaneous actions: *as*

Action 1   The numbers of Portuguese increased.
Action 2   The power of the Arabs was reduced.

As the numbers of Portuguese increased, the power of the Arabs was reduced.

c   To show an action and its limit: *until*

Action   The Portuguese ruled the city.
Limit   The Germans defeated them.

The Portuguese ruled the city *until* the Germans defeated them.

When time clauses come at the beginning of a sentence, they are followed by a comma (,). For example:

Until the Germans defeated them, the Portuguese ruled the city.

Exercise 5

Link each pair of events according to the symbol given. For example:

a   The Wright brothers took off in 1908.
b   A new age of flying began.

When the Wright brothers took off in 1908, a new age of flying began.

1
a   The century progressed.
b   Longer and longer distances were covered.

2
a   The Second World War ended.
b   Jet airliners were built.

3
a   Man had flown only in balloons.
b   The Wright brothers' flight.

4
a   Radar was introduced.
b   Flying became safer.

5
a   The First World War broke out in 1914.
b   More powerful planes, including four-engined bombers, were built.

6
a   The War ended.
b   These bombers were developed into the first airliners.

7
a   Radar was invented.
b   The Second World War broke out.

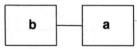

Put the completed sentences in the correct order and combine them into a paragraph. You may add examples and further details of your own to improve the paragraph.

Section 3 Describing graphs

Exercise 6
This graph shows the average number of cigarettes smoked per head of population in a European country over a period of sixty years. Study it carefully.

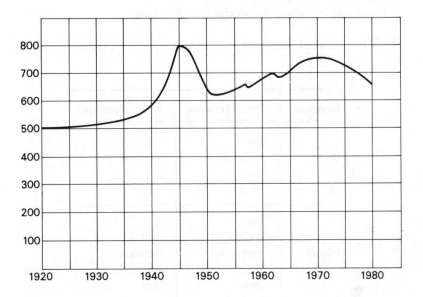

Write a sentence to describe the graph for the following periods:

1   1920 –1930
2   1945–1950
3   1968–1972
4   1956–1958

Compare your sentences with those of another student.

Comment
Graphs are a way of showing change visually. They are often used in Physics, the Life Sciences, Economics and the Social Sciences and are an economic way of presenting information.

Useful language   Describing change

Look at the period 1920–1930 in the graph. We can describe this part of the graph in two ways:

1   By using a verb of change. For example:
     Cigarette smoking *rose.*

2   By using a related noun.
     There was *a rise* in cigarette smoking.

You can add an adverb or an adjective to describe the rate of change. For example:
     Cigarette smoking rose *gradually.*
     There was a *gradual* rise in cigarette smoking.

Study this table of verbs and related nouns used in graphs.

Direction	Verb of change	Noun of change
UP	rise increase climb go up	rise increase – –
DOWN	fall decline decrease dip drop go down	fall decline decrease dip drop –
LEVEL	level out not change remain steady	levelling out no change –

Learn these adjectives used to describe the rate of change. Add *-ly* to form the adverb. For example:
     gradual   gradually

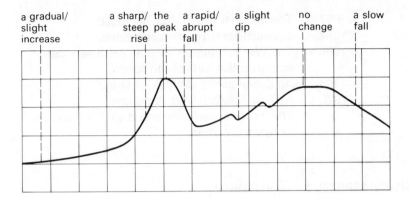

a gradual/ slight increase   a sharp/ steep rise   the peak   a rapid/ abrupt fall   a slight dip   no change   a slow fall

Exercise 7

Rewrite each of these sentences to make a sentence of similar meaning using a noun of change.

1 Between 1920 and 1930 cigarette smoking increased gradually.
2 Between 1945 and 1950 cigarette smoking fell sharply.
3 Between 1968 and 1972 cigarette consumption did not change.
4 Between 1956 and 1958 cigarette smoking dipped slightly.

Exercise 8

Describe the graph on page 69 for these periods using either a verb or a noun of change.

1 1940–1945
2 1972–1980
3 1961–1964
4 1951–1956

Compare your answers with those of other students.

Exercise 9

Try to guess the reasons for some of the changes in the graph. Then study the information which follows. Select the information which you think gives the most likely reasons for the changes.

1920's   Men changed from pipes to cigarettes.
          Women started to smoke.
          Radio became more popular.
1930's   Many people were without work.
1939   The Second World War started.
          Soldiers were able to buy cigarettes cheaply.
1945   The War ended.
          Only essential things were imported.
1951   Import bans were lifted.

1957	The tax on tobacco was increased.
1962	Tobacco tax was again increased.
1960's	The War in Vietnam became more serious.
	Man travelled further into space.
1968	An anti-smoking campaign started.
1970's	Artificial tobacco was introduced.
	The link between cancer and smoking became increasingly clear.

Useful language   Giving reasons

Look at this example:

Cigarette smoking rose after 1939 *because* the Second World War started.

You can also use *because of*. This must be followed by a noun phrase. For example:

Cigarette smoking rose after 1939 *because of* the start of the Second World War.

Exercise 10
Add the reasons for each of the changes you described in Exercises 7 and 8. Then write a description of the complete graph.

Exercise 11
Study these two graphs. The first shows the number of television sets licensed in a European country over a period of 35 years. The second graph shows changes in cinema and football match attendances over the same period in the same country.

Graph 1

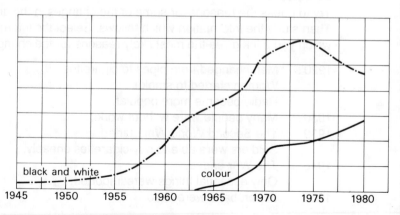

Graph 2

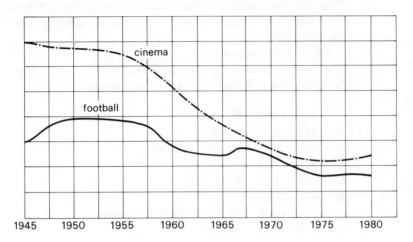

1945   1950   1955   1960   1965   1970   1975   1980

Look at the information below. Which information provides the most likely reasons for the changes shown in Graph 1? Which for Graph 2?

1945	Very few television sets were made. Only a few big cities could receive television. Professional football started again now the war was over.
From 1955	Cheaper television sets were introduced. People had more money to spend.
From 1958	More football matches were shown on television.
1960	The whole country could receive television.
1963	Separate licences for colour and black and white sets were introduced.
1965	The rules were changed to allow quite new films to be shown on television.
1968	A campaign was started to identify people using sets without a licence.
1970's	Violence among the crowds at football matches increased.
1971	The cost of colour licences was increased sharply.
1972	More money was put into the film industry to improve the standard of films.

Exercise 12

Describe the changes in the periods below. Refer to the graphs indicated. Add reasons using the information given in Exercise 11. For example,
  1968–1970 television
The number of sets licensed between 1968 and 1970 rose sharply because of a campaign to identify unlicensed sets.

1   1945–1955   television
2   1945–1950   football
3   1968–1975   colour television
4   1970–1980   cinema
5   1955–1960   television
6   1970–1980   football
7   1960–1968   black and white television
8   1958–1965   football

Exercise 13

Write a brief description with this title: *Changes In Leisure Activities*. Use the information contained in the graphs and explanatory data given. Before you write, make an outline plan and decide how many paragraphs to include.

Section 4 Homework exercises

Select an exercise from this section which is related to your own field of study or which is of special interest to you. You should complete the exercise in your own time.

1   *General knowledge – Education in Ubanda*
   This graph shows the percentage of school students studying three languages in Ubanda, a former Portuguese colony. The languages are: Portuguese, Kibanda and English. Some of the information given on page 75 helps to explain the changes in the graph but not all of the information is relevant. Using the graph and the information which is relevant, write a full description of changes in language study in Ubandan schools.

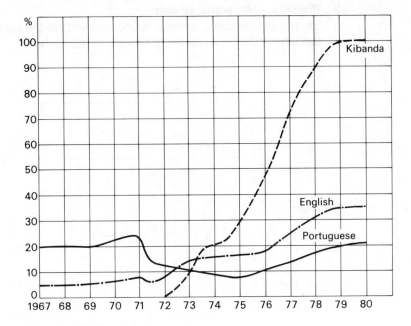

1966 The President of Portugal visited Ubanda.
1969 The colonial government began long-term preparations for independence.
There were riots in the capital.
1971 Independence was seized by force.
Diplomatic relations with Portugal were cut.
Many schools abandoned the teaching of Portuguese.
1972 Kibanda, a lingua franca, was introduced in secondary schools.
A programme of land reform was started.
1974 There was a military coup in Portugal.
Kibanda was made the national language. It was taught in all schools.
1975 The Trans-Ubandan railway line was opened.
Diplomatic relations with Portugal were resumed.
Portuguese aid was started.
1976 Ubanda joined the Trans-African Trade Community.
Most other members are English-speaking.
1978 The first President of Ubanda died.

2   *Physics – Hot water system*

a   Study this diagram. Describe the components of the system and say where they are located in relation to each other.

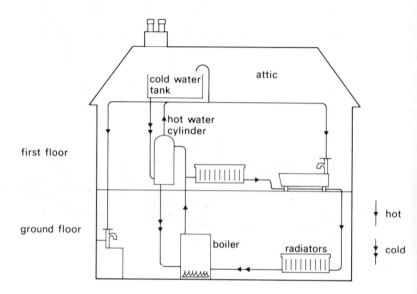

b   Now describe the flow of water through the system by linking each group of sentences into one sentence. Use time clauses or any other methods of linking sentences you have studied.

1   The boiler is turned on. The water next to the heat source becomes warm.
2   The water heats. The water expands.
3   The hot water is less dense. The hot water rises into the hot water cylinder.
4   The hot water rises. The hot water is replaced by cooler water.
5   These movements continue. All the water in the cylinder is at the required temperature.
6   Some of the hot water is drawn off. Cold water flows into the cylinder from the roof tank.
7   The boiler also provides hot water. The hot water is for central heating.
8   The water heats. The water rises by convection through the radiators.
9   The hot water flows through the radiators. The hot water loses heat.
10 The hot water loses heat. The hot water becomes denser and sinks back to the boiler. In the boiler the water is again heated.
11 Usually a pump is fitted to the system. The pump speeds the flow of hot water.

3 *Geology – Coal formation*

Combine the information in each diagram and in the text to write a brief description of how coal was formed millions of years ago. Remember to use the past tense.

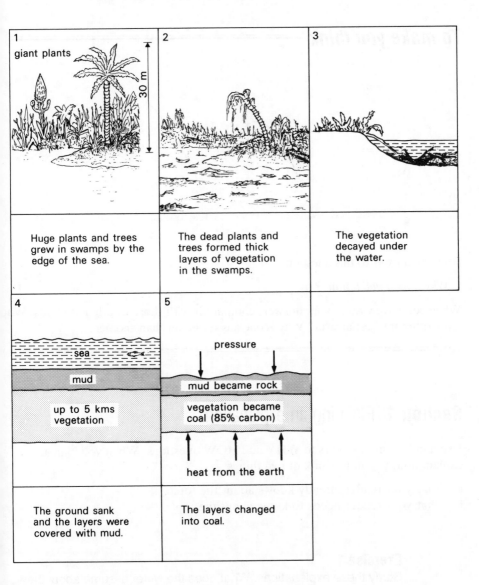

1 giant plants

30 m

Huge plants and trees grew in swamps by the edge of the sea.

2

The dead plants and trees formed thick layers of vegetation in the swamps.

3

The vegetation decayed under the water.

4

sea

mud

up to 5 kms vegetation

The ground sank and the layers were covered with mud.

5

pressure

mud became rock

vegetation became coal (85% carbon)

heat from the earth

The layers changed into coal.

6 Writing explanations

To make you think

Write an answer to this question:

Why does a ball bounce?

When you have written your answer, compare it with those of other students. Who has written the best answer? Why is one answer better than another?

Section 1 Planning an explanation

Explanations are answers to WHY and HOW questions. When you plan an explanation, you must think of two things:

a   what your reader already knows about the topic.
b   what your reader needs to know about the topic.

Exercise 1
Study these explanations. What does the writer assume about the reader's knowledge and needs in each case? Which explanation best matches your knowledge and needs?

1   Balls bounce because they are made of rubber.
2   Balls bounce because they are made of rubber, which is an elastic substance.
3   Balls bounce because they are made of rubber, which is an

elastic substance. Such materials try to regain their original shape when they are distorted.

4   Balls bounce because they are made of rubber, which is an elastic substance. Such materials try to regain their original shape when they are distorted. When a ball hits a hard surface, it is flattened. The elasticity of the rubber then causes it to regain its original shape.

Exercise 2

You can test how good an explanation is for you by noting how many **How** and **Why** questions are NOT answered. Study this set of instructions for victims of poisoning. Then list the **How** and **Why** questions you would like answered. Your first question might be:

Why should artificial respiration be started immediately?

When you have completed your list, find out how many of your questions another student can answer.

1   If the victim is not breathing, give him artificial respiration immediately.
2   Call a doctor.
3   If he seems likely to vomit, place him on his stomach with his head to one side.
4   If he is conscious, ask him what he has taken. Look for bottles, tablets or the smell of chemicals.
5   Keep him warm.
6   Do not leave him before the doctor arrives.

Now study the second set of instructions which contain explanations.

1   If the victim is not breathing, give him artificial respiration immediately. *Lack of oxygen can cause brain damage within three minutes.*
2   Call a doctor *to obtain expert help.*
3   If he seems likely to vomit, place him on his stomach with his head to one side *so that he will not inhale any vomit which might choke him.*
4   If he is conscious, ask him what he has taken. Look for bottles, tablets or the smell of any chemical *as this will make it easier to identify the poison and start the correct treatment.*
5   Keep him warm *to limit the effects of shock.*
6   Do not leave him before the doctor arrives *because his condition may worsen quickly.*

How many of your questions are answered?

Useful language   Answering **Why** and **How** questions

Remember these ways of answering **Why** questions (See Unit 5):

Keep him warm
a   *to limit the effects of shock.*
b   *so that the effects of shock are limited.*
c   *because you must limit the effects of shock.*

Remember this way of answering **How** questions:

Keep him warm *by wrapping him in a blanket.*

Exercise 3

Try to answer the **Why** and **How** questions in these instructions. The illustrations will help you but you will also have to add information of your own. Work in pairs.

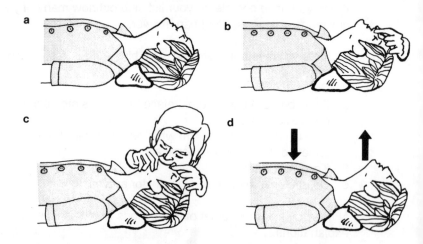

1   Start artificial respiration as quickly as possible. **Why?**
2   Ensure the victim has a clear airway. **Why? How?**
3   Seal the nostrils. **How? Why?**
4   Place your wide-open mouth right round the victim's to make an air-tight seal (**Why?**) and blow hard. **Why?**
5   Remove your mouth and watch the chest fall.
6   Repeat about six times quickly using oxygen-rich air from your mouth. **Why?**
7   Repeat and continue the action at your natural rate of breathing. **Why?**

When you have both agreed on the answers, rewrite each instruction to include your answers. For example:

Start artificial respiration as quickly as possible *because delay may cause brain damage.*

Exercise 4

Look at the tasks below. Choose one of the tasks and write instructions for it. When you have written your instructions, compare them with those of another student who has written on the same topic. Ask the other student **Why** and **How** questions about any point you do not understand.

1　Starting a car.
2　Stopping a nose bleed.
3　Repairing a bicycle puncture.
4　Removing a stamp from an envelope without damaging it.
5　Recording with a tape recorder.
6　Operating any instrument or piece of equipment you are familiar with.

Section 2 Supporting an explanation

Exercise 5

Study this general statement and the statements which support it.

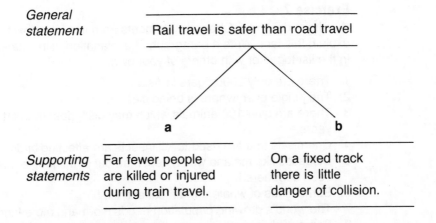

General statement　　Rail travel is safer than road travel

a　　　　　　　　　　b

Supporting statements　Far fewer people are killed or injured during train travel.　　On a fixed track there is little danger of collision.

Which supporting statement is better as an explanation of the general statement?

Comment

In explanations you must support general statements which your reader may not understand. Statement (a) merely rephrases the general statement whereas statement (b) provides a reason. When writing explanations make sure your supporting statements provide reasons.

Exercise 6

Which supporting statement, (a) or (b), would you use to explain each of these general statements?

1   Many towns grew up near rivers.
a   London, New York and Amsterdam were built on river banks.
b   The river provided water, transport and, later, power.

2   Wood is a useful building material.
a   Wood is used for doors, roofs and floors.
b   For its weight, wood is exceptionally strong.

3   Fruit and vegetables are essential for health.
a   Fruit and vegetables contain vitamin C.
b   Ships always carry supplies of fruit and vegetables to keep the crew healthy.

4   Much of North Africa is desert.
a   Very little rain falls in North Africa.
b   Very little will grow in North Africa.

5   Gold was used for money in many parts of the world.
a   Gold is a rare metal and it does not corrode.
b   Gold coins were made in Europe, Asia and America.

Exercise 7

Wildlife is declining. Choose statements from the list below to explain this fact. Write a paragraph of explanation using statements in the list together with others of your own.

1   There are only 2000 tigers in Asia.
2   The jungle everywhere is being cleared.
3   There are over 100 animals which may disappear in the next 25 years.
4   Chemicals that are used to kill insects are affecting birds.
5   Diseases like malaria which kept man out of the jungle have been conquered.
6   Some kinds of whale are almost extinct.
7   The world's growing population needs more and more land.
8   Some wild animals, such as the whale, are being overhunted.

Section 3   Cause and effect in explanations

Exercise 8

Study this list. What relationship can you see between the items? Put the list in the correct order to show this relationship.

careless driving   too much alcohol
accidents   drunkenness

Useful language   Cause and effect 1

Cause and effect relationships like those above are common in explanations. You can link a cause and an effect when both are noun phrases in the following ways:

1   If you want to mention the *cause* first –

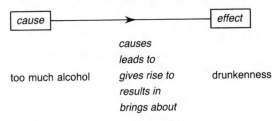

| | causes | |
| too much alcohol | leads to
gives rise to
results in
brings about | drunkenness |

2   If you want to mention the *effect* first –

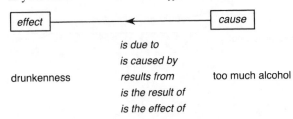

| | is due to | |
| drunkenness | is caused by
results from
is the result of
is the effect of | too much alcohol |

When an effect may have several causes or a cause several effects, you add *may*. For example:
   Pollution *may* be caused by smoke.
   Smoking *may* cause heart disease.

Exercise 9

Look at these lists. Items on the left can be causes or effects of items on the right. But the items are mixed up. Copy the lists and join items with an arrow to show which is the cause and which is the effect, like this:

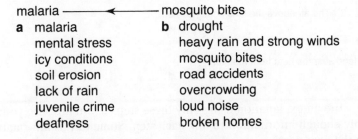

a	malaria	b	drought
	mental stress		heavy rain and strong winds
	icy conditions		mosquito bites
	soil erosion		road accidents
	lack of rain		overcrowding
	juvenile crime		loud noise
	deafness		broken homes

Now write sentences to show the relationship. For example:
   Malaria *is caused by* mosquito bites.

Exercise 10

Study this diagram which explains why the wind blows from the sea to the land during the day. How much of the diagram can you understand? Write a brief explanation.

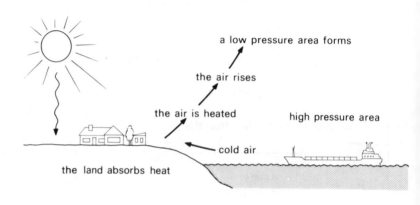

Comment

The explanation consists of a series of cause and effect steps. Here are some of them:

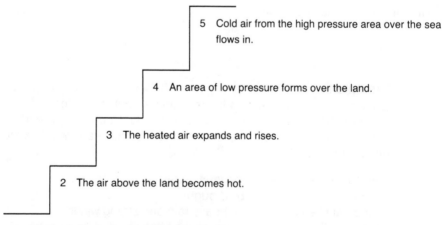

You can write an explanation using only these steps if you are sure your reader can supply enough information to link each step. Some of this information is given on the next page.

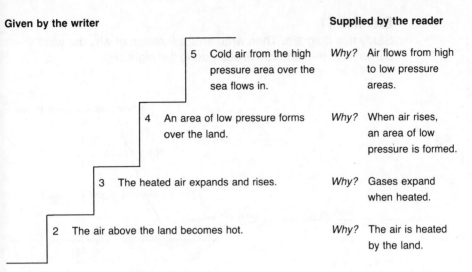

Given by the writer   **Supplied by the reader**

5   Cold air from the high   *Why?*   Air flows from high
    pressure area over the   to low pressure
    sea flows in.   areas.

4   An area of low pressure forms *Why?*   When air rises,
    over the land.   an area of low
                                            pressure is formed.

3   The heated air expands and rises. *Why?*   Gases expand
                                                when heated.

2   The air above the land becomes hot. *Why?*   The air is heated
                                                  by the land.

1   The land absorbs heat from the sun.

When you write an explanation with cause and effect steps, you must try to estimate what your reader already knows. Otherwise you may miss out important steps and the explanation will not be understood.

Useful language   Cause and effect 2

Here are some other ways of linking causes and effects:

1   *Because, therefore* (See Unit 1)

| effect | ← | cause |

The air above the land becomes hot *because* the land absorbs heat from the sun.

| cause | → | effect |

The land absorbs heat from the sun. *Therefore* the air above it becomes hot.

Instead of *therefore*, you can also use *consequently* or *as a result*. For example:

The air above the land becomes hot, *consequently* the heated air expands and rises.

The heated air expands and rises. *As a result*, an area of low pressure forms over the land.

If the link between cause and effect is obvious, no connecting word is needed.

2   *Cause* (someone/something) *to*. For example:

The heated air expands and rises. This *causes* an area of low pressure *to* form over the land.

The heated air expands and rises, *causing* an area of low pressure *to* form over the land.

Exercise 11

Study this diagram. Then write an explanation of why the wind blows from the land to the sea during the night.

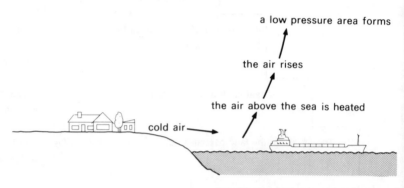

a low pressure area forms

the air rises

the air above the sea is heated

cold air ⟶

the sea retains the heat longer than the land

Exercise 12

Study this problem and try to write a short explanation of your own. Compare your explanation with those suggested by other members of your class.

Imagine a tall black cylinder standing on a white table in front of you. No one is near the table and there is nothing on the table except the cylinder which stands stark and alone. About twenty minutes pass. Suddenly, without warning, the cylinder falls over with a crash. Why? No one has gone near it. Nothing has been seen to happen. There is no sound except the crash of the falling cylinder. You are asked to try and understand what has happened and to write down your explanation. But you have only ten minutes in which to think of an explanation – and you are not allowed to examine the cylinder in any way.

Exercise 13

These diagrams illustrate four different explanations. Each involves cause and effect steps. Work in groups. Try to explain one of the diagrams in writing. If you think the diagram does not give a good solution to the black cylinder problem, explain why it does not. When your group has written its explanation, exchange it for that of another group. Decide how good each explanation is. Write a comparison and contrast of any two of the explanations.

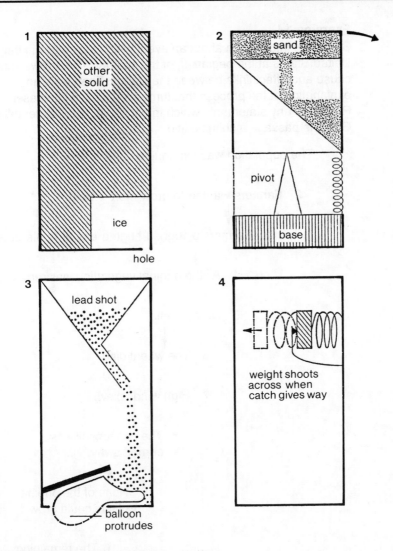

Guiding the reader   Rephrasing

You learned in Unit 2 that you can help your reader by defining unknown terms and by giving examples to illustrate a difficult point. If you write something which is not easy to understand, you can also help your reader by repeating it in a different way, to give him a second chance to understand. Study these examples:

1   London, New York and Amsterdam were all riparian settlements. *In other words*, they grew up along river banks.
2   Iron was the medium of exchange in parts of Africa, *that is*, it was used as money.

Note that these words are used to introduce rephrasings:
  that is (i.e.)
  in other words

Exercise 14

Study this information about an event which took place in the
United States at the beginning of the century. The arrows show
cause and effect links between the stages. Then write an
explanation of the process that turned fertile land into desert.
Rephrase any statements which might cause your reader difficulty.
Give the passage a suitable title.

1 The population was expanding.

2 Farmers wanted to grow more wheat.

3 Farmers ploughed huge areas of fertile grassland.

4 All the original vegetation was removed.

5 No rain fell.

6 The wheat died.

7 High winds blew.

8 The rich topsoil was
carried away.

9 None of the original
plants could grow.

10 The remaining
soil was very
poor.

11 The area
became
a desert.

Section 4 Homework exercises

Write an explanation of one of the topics in this section. Choose
one from your own field of study or one which is of special interest
to you. You may add any information of your own or from reference
books.

Make sure your explanation answers the WHY questions your readers will want to ask. Some of the topics involve cause and effect steps. Ensure that your readers will be able to follow the steps in your explanation without having to provide too much information themselves.

1 *General knowledge – How does erosion occur?*
   Use the information in the diagrams and text to explain how erosion occurs. You will have to complete the texts below each *After* picture first.

Water erosion

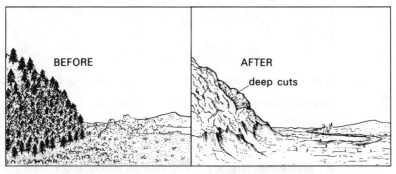

Trees cover the hillside.	The trees are cut down for firewood.
Some of the rain is absorbed by the trees.	The rain is not absorbed ...
The rest of the rain runs slowly down the hillside without removing top soil.	The rain runs quickly down the hillside, removing ...

Wind erosion

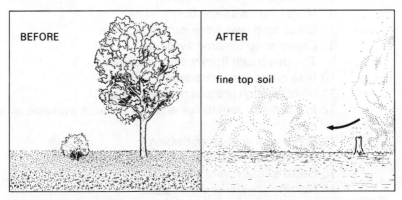

The roots of grass and bushes bind the soil together.	The vegetation is cleared and the land ploughed.
Trees break the force of the wind.	The roots ......
	The trees ....
	The top soil is blown away.

Overgrazing

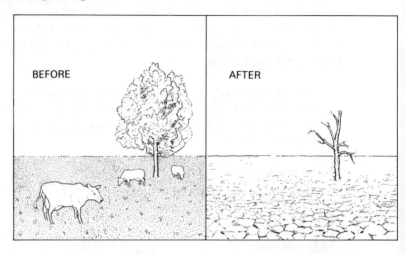

A few cows and goats are kept.

The grass and other vegetation can replace itself.

Too many cows and goats are kept.

The grass ......
The land ....

2   *Medicine, History – The Health Revolution*
Study this list of the causes of the health revolution in Europe which took place between about 1860 and 1920.

1 The birth rate fell.
2 Refrigerated ships were introduced.
3 Infection was reduced.
4 Nutrition improved.
5 Personal hygiene got better.
6 More hospitals were built.
7 Clean food laws were introduced.
8 Cheap soap became available.
9 The death rate from many diseases fell.
10 New drugs were introduced.
11 Immunisation programmes were started.
12 Fresh meat, vegetables and fruit became available all the year round.
13 There was less overcrowding.
14 Food became cleaner and therefore safer.
15 Better houses were built.
16 Nursing standards were raised.
17 Cheap cotton clothes became available.
18 Living conditions improved.

Put the causes into groups by copying the diagram and writing the number of each cause in the correct circle. Some have been entered to help you.

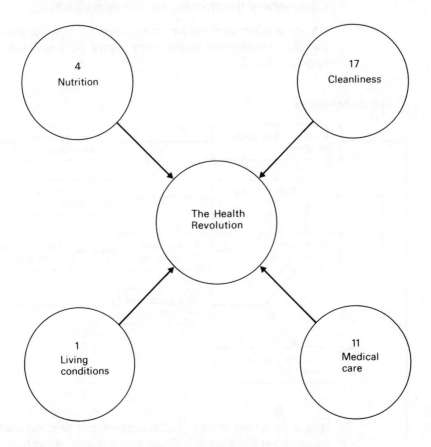

The causes are related. They form cause and effect chains. For example:

2–12–4

Find another cause and effect chain within the groups and join them to make a paragraph for each group. For example:

Nutrition: Refrigerated ships were introduced which meant that fresh meat, vegetables and fruit became available all the year round. As a result, nutrition improved.

Arrange your paragraphs in the most effective order to make an explanation of the health revolution.

3   *Economics – Slump-boom-slump*

Study this diagram. It shows the stages through which a country's economy goes from slump to boom. Write an explanation of the process. You can begin like this:

If there is a low demand for goods, firms cut costs and prices, therefore housewives spend more money. As a result, demand begins to rise.....

(a) SLUMP-BOOM

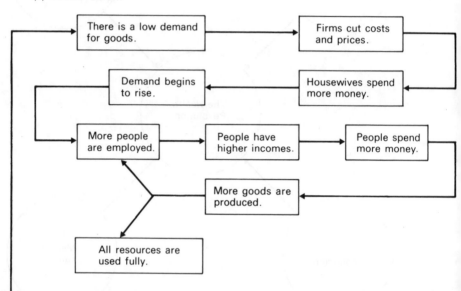

Now write an explanation of the boom-slump process which is illustrated in this diagram. Show how a slump can in turn lead back to a boom.

(b) BOOM-SLUMP

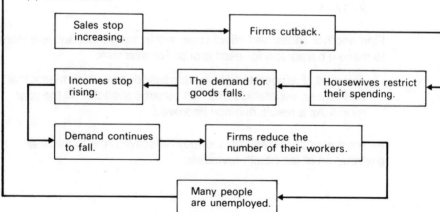

7 Writing arguments

To make you think

Write down the main points you would make in an argument to persuade another student to adopt one of these careers.

1	actor/actress	5	engineer
2	sea captain	6	politician
3	doctor	7	librarian
4	teacher	8	soldier

List the points in the best order in your notebook. Add supporting reasons for each point where you can.

Now pass your list to another student. He will try to argue against each point you make. When he has finished, read his replies and consider how your argument could be improved.

Section 1 Planning an argument: Facts and opinions

Exercise 1

Consider these statements. Which would you accept without argument? Why would you accept them and not the others?

1. Poverty is caused by laziness.
2. Intelligence is affected by the environment.
3. The Earth revolves round the Sun.
4. Competition in sport encourages violence.
5. Materials expand when they are heated.

Comment

The first step in planning an argument is to list the points you wish to make. Some of these may be facts. Some may be opinions. Facts are statements which are known to be true. Opinions are personal beliefs which may or may not be true. Both facts and opinions are used in arguments but it is important to distinguish between them. Your reader will not be convinced by an argument consisting only of opinions.

Exercise 2
Which of these statements are facts and which are opinions? Compare your answers with those of another student and be prepared to justify your choice.

1   Man is the most intelligent of the animals.
2   Nuclear power is the answer to the world's energy problems.
3   Carelessness is the cause of many accidents.
4   Most unemployed people have no work because they do not want to work.
5   Pets in the home are a health risk.
6   The movement of people from rural areas to towns must be stopped to avoid future problems.

Exercise 3
Write one factual statement and one opinion on each of the following topics. When you have completed them, exchange them with another student and see whether he or she would agree with you.

1   a historical person e.g. Stalin
2   modern education
3   sport
4   cars in cities
5   health

Exercise 4
Go back to Exercise 2. Select any one of the topics and list the main points you would use in an argument on that topic. When you have completed your list, check which are facts and which are opinions.

Section 2 Supporting an argument

Exercise 5
Which of the statements (a) to (e) provides the best support for this statement?
Smoking is harmful to health.

a   Smoking is a silly habit.
b   Ten times as many smokers get lung cancer as non-smokers.
c   People smoke much more when they are worried.
d   Smoking makes you unhealthy.
e   There is a link between lung cancer and cigarette smoking.

Comment

When you write an explanation, you must try to make your reader *understand* your points. When you write an argument, you must try to *convince* your reader that your points are correct. To do so you must provide strong support for your arguments. (a) is an opinion, (b) is a relevant fact, (c) is a fact but it is irrelevant to this argument, (d) is merely the main statement repeated in different words, (e) is a relevant fact but too general to be useful.

Relevant facts provide the best support in arguments. Opinions should not be used to support other opinions.

Guiding the reader   Reinforcement

Study these statements:

1 Motorcycles are preferable to cars.
a   They use less petrol.
b   They cause little air pollution.

Both (a) and (b) support statement 1. (b) provides additional support to make the argument stronger. It *reinforces* (a). You can show this by using these expressions:

> *furthermore*
> *besides*
> *in addition*
> *moreover*

For example:

> Motorcycles are preferable to cars because they use less petrol. *Furthermore*, they cause little air pollution.

Exercise 6

Complete these sets of statements using a reinforcing idea of your own. Then link the statements in each set together. Use the expressions given above.

1 Education for women is a waste of time.
a   Most women become housewives.
b

2 Education for women is essential.
a   Women have the greatest influence on the family.
b

3   Country life is better than city life.
a   The air in the country is cleaner.
b

4   City life is better than country life.
a   There are more things to do in the city.
b

Exercise 7
Study this argument about prisons. Which of the main points in it
are facts and which are opinions? Which points are used to support
the main points?

1   Prisons are an unsatisfactory way of dealing with those who
break the law. 2   They do not deter and they may not even punish.
3   Prisons provide an opportunity for prisoners to improve their
criminal knowledge. 4   They serve as training schools in crime.
5   In addition, prisons are expensive. 6   Thus the honest citizen
pays taxes to support a system which may help to increase crime.

Exercise 8
Which of these statements would you use to support the main
points in the argument on prisons? Rewrite the argument using the
statements you have selected. You can add information of your
own. Use reinforcement expressions where necessary.

a   Sentences are reviewed after a prisoner has served two years.
b   More than 35% of prisoners break the law again after their
    release from prison.
c   Prisoners are allowed visitors and letters.
d   Prisoners can earn a small sum of money by working in prison.
e   Modern prisons provide libraries and sports facilities for
    prisoners.
f   Prisoners sometimes attack their guards.
g   Young prisoners often meet more experienced criminals and
    learn from them.
h   It costs more than £150 a week to keep a prisoner in jail.

Exercise 9
Look at the statements and the information below them. Choose the
relevant information to support the statements. You can add
information of your own.

1 *The world's wealth is badly distributed.*

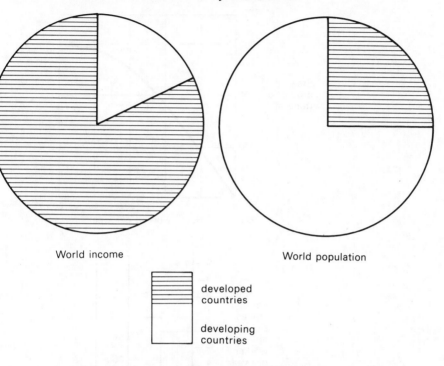

World income

World population

developed
countries

developing
countries

2 *Rail transport is preferable to road transport.*

	Road	Rail
Energy used	300 units	100 units
Peak noise levels	truck 88–92 decibels	train 90–92 decibels
Deaths per 1000 million passenger miles	31	8.6
Serious injuries per 1000 million passenger miles	367	12.4
Annual tonnage of goods carried	3370 million tonnes	750 million tonnes

3   *A 45-hour working week is too long.*

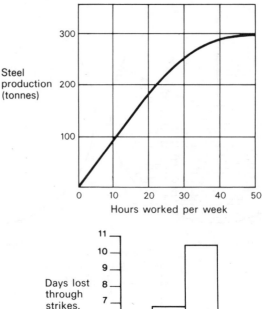

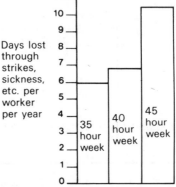

Section 3 Organising an argument

Exercise 10

Study this list of points on international languages. Put them in order to make an argument in favour of English as a world language. When you have finished, compare your answer with your neighbours.

a   In English, the verb changes only in the third person.
b   British colonies were more widespread than French.
c   English is a better choice than French for a world language.
d   Nouns and adjectives must agree in French.
e   Today English is spoken in all parts of the world.
f   English was taught in all British colonies.
g   English is easier than French.

Comment

A good argument has to be effectively organised so that your reader can follow the chain of argument and be convinced by it. Here is one possible structure for the argument above:

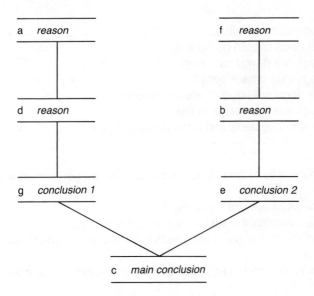

This method leads up to the main point. Another way would be to start with the main point and then provide the supporting argument.

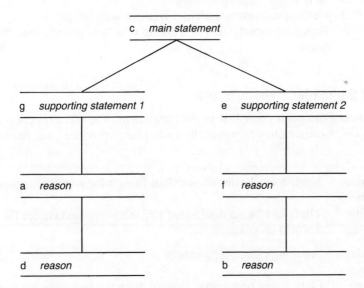

Exercise 11

Study these groups of sentences. Identify the main point in each group and then organise the sentences into an effective argument. Draw a diagram to show the organisation of the argument.

1
a Dogs carry disease.
b Pet dogs should be banned.
c Dogs are dangerous to man.
d Dogs may attack people.
e Pet dogs eat large quantities of food.
f Dogs are expensive to keep.
g People buy beds and even toys for dogs.

2
a Success in exams depends on the student performing well on one day only.
b Exams cause great anxiety.
c The examination system should be changed.
d The student is not given credit for good work throughout the year.
e Some students do not perform well because they are anxious.

3
a Many people in the country areas of developing nations cannot get clean water.
b About 8 million children die every year from disease caught from dirty water.
c Dirty water causes ill health.
d Health programmes should improve water supplies.
e Providing piped water is a cheap way to improve a nation's health.

Guiding the reader   Adding emphasis

When you put the main point first in your argument, you often repeat it in a stronger and more emphatic form at the end to help convince your reader. For example:

1 *Opening sentence*   English is a better choice than French for a world language.

   Closing sentence   There can be no doubt that English is the best choice for a world language.

2 *Opening sentence*   Smoking causes lung cancer.

   Closing sentence   Only a fool or a smoker would deny the link between smoking and cancer of the lung.

Exercise 12

Link each group of sentences in Exercise 11 into a paragraph using connecting words where necessary. Where appropriate, add an emphatic closing sentence of your own.

Exercise 13

This outline plan shows the main points for an argument with the title: *Choosing an international language for the 21st century.*

a   Various languages may seem suitable but none is perfect.
b   English is the best choice.
c   An international language must satisfy several criteria.
d   An artificial language is not a solution.

First write down the points in the best order. Leave space to add supporting information after each point. Look at the information below. Select information which will support each point, and write it under each point. Some of the information is not relevant.

Source 1   Major world languages

Language	Number of speakers	Distribution
Arabic	110,000,000	Middle East, North Africa, Sudan
Chinese (8 main dialects)	1,000,000,000	China, parts of S E Asia
English	320,000,000	Britain, North America, Australasia, Africa, India, etc.
Russian	145,000,000	USSR
Spanish	160,000,000	Spain, Central and South America

Source 2   Artificial languages
A number of artificial languages have been developed to try to solve the world's communication problems by providing a language which is easy to learn and can express all the concepts needed for modern life. The oldest is Volapuk. The only one to have much success is Esperanto which claims 10 million speakers. It has a limited vocabulary and its grammar has no irregularities. Like other

artificial languages it is based on Western European languages so that for learners whose mother tongue is not a European language, it is not particularly easy to learn. There are very few books and almost no films or newspapers in Esperanto.

Source 3   The English language
A Germanic language spoken as the main language in the British Isles, USA, Canada, New Zealand and Australia and known in many areas once under British control. Spoken by 10% or more of the population of over 30 countries as a second language. The most important of the international languages. The official language of the sea and air. The most common language for all publications, especially scientific. Around 50% of writing on science is in English. Its development is divided into three stages: Old English (450–1100), Middle English (1100–1500) and Modern English (1500 to present).

From each point and its supporting information, write a paragraph. You can add information of your own.

Exercise 14
Write an argument in favour of choosing your own language, or any other language besides English, as the international language for the 21st Century.

Guiding the reader   Bridging sentences

Bridging sentences remind the reader of what has gone before and introduce what is to come. Look at the outline of a text arguing for the preservation of the tiger.

Section 1   Reasons for the fall in the number of tigers.
Section 2   Arguments for preserving the tiger.
Section 3   Ways of preserving the tiger.

Study these bridging sentences. They link Sections 1 and 2:

1   Having established the reasons for the decline of the tiger, let us consider why we should try to stop the decline.
2   Given these reasons for the tiger's decline, what case is there for preserving the tiger?

What bridging sentences can you suggest to link Sections 2 and 3?

Go back to Exercise 13 and add a suitable bridging sentence between the sections.

Section 4 Refuting an argument

Exercise 15

Study this argument about nuclear power. Is it *for* or *against* nuclear power?

1   The increase in the use of nuclear power should be stopped.
2   Nuclear power stations are extremely dangerous. 3   In 1979 a station in the USA went out of control and thousands had to leave their homes. 4   The waste from nuclear power stations can be dangerous to man for thousands of years. 5   Nuclear stations are unnecessary. 6   The demand for electricity in the West is increasing very slowly and can be met by existing stations. 7   If extra power is needed, it should be provided by wind or tidal power stations. 8   They are safe and there is no danger of pollution.
9   For these reasons all work on nuclear power stations must be halted immediately.

Now copy this diagram and write down the sentence numbers of the main points and the supporting information in the correct places to show the structure of the argument. Identify the type of statement in each case. Some spaces have been filled and labelled for you.

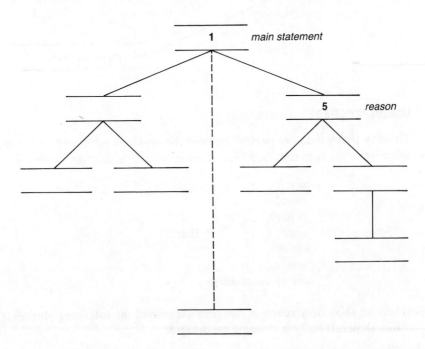

Which of the statements are facts and which are opinions? Are all the supporting statements relevant?

Comment

When you want to *refute*, that is argue against, an argument, you should consider its weak points. It is not enough to argue against the *main* points only. You should also try to argue against the *supporting* reasons.

Study this example:

1   The Flat Earth Society claim that the Earth is flat. 2   They say that we would all fall off if it were round. 3   This is nonsense. 4   We know that the world is round because, if we travel far enough in any direction, we will eventually arrive back where we started. 5   We do not fall off because we are held by gravity to the Earth.

This paragraph has the following structure:

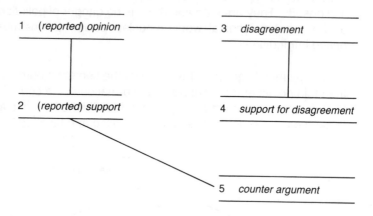

Useful language   Disagreeing

To show that we do not personally hold the opinions we intend to refute, we often write them as reported speech using one of these verbs or phrases:

Some people
say
assert
believe
state
claim
maintain
are of the opinion
that . . . . .

When we show disagreement, we may use one of the following phrases. Our choice depends on how strongly we disagree.

This is unlikely to be true.
They would seem to be mistaken.
These views are open to doubt.
Serious doubts can be raised against this.

Exercise 16
Write a paragraph to refute each of these arguments.

1   Bus drivers are more likely to suffer from heart disease than bus conductors. We can conclude that sitting down is less healthy than walking up and down.
2   Sales of tinned pet food are high in the poorest areas of American cities. It is clear that poor Americans are particularly fond of animals.
3   A survey of cinema audiences shows that most are in the age groups 18–25 and 45 and over. It is obvious that modern films do not appeal to those in the 25–45 age group.
4   Compared with 1930, the number of lives lost through plane crashes has increased four times. From this we can see that modern aircraft are much more dangerous than the early planes.

Exercise 17
Each of these opinions has supporters. Choose one you do NOT agree with and provide evidence of your own to write a brief argument against it.

1   Women are inferior to men.
2   The Earth is visited regularly by people from other planets.
3   Drinking alcohol is evil.
4   All forms of government are unacceptable.

Exercise 18
Write an argument in favour of one of these topics and an argument against the other. When you have finished, exchange with a student who has made the opposite choice from you. Try to write arguments refuting his work.

1   Everyone should be paid the same wage.
2   You should be free to spend your money as you wish.

Section 5 Homework exercises

1   ***General knowledge – Nuclear power***
    Select from these sources as much information as you can to refute the points made in the argument against nuclear power stations in Exercise 15. You may also add extra information of your own. Make sure all the data you select is relevant.

Source 1　Nuclear Safety
Nuclear stations are completely safe. They cannot blow up like a bomb. The reactor is surrounded by a 3.5 metre thick concrete wall. The station is protected by three different automatic systems which close down the reactor if an accident happens. Radiation from nuclear stations is tiny, only 0.2% of the radiation in the air. Workers in nuclear stations are much less at risk than in most other industries.

Source 2　Radiation hazards (REMS)
0.125　average background radiation
0.17　maximum exposure allowed to the public
0.5　maximum level at nuclear power stations
1.35　highest natural level (Madras, India)
5　maximum dose for radiation workers
500　always fatal

Source 3　Advantages of nuclear power
Nuclear power is cheap, only half the price of electricity generated from oil. Only small quantities of fuel are required. 10 tonnes of nuclear fuel will provide a month's electricity for a city of half a million. To generate the same power would need 75,000 tonnes of coal.

2　**Economics – Small versus large companies**
Study these facts from a survey of small and large companies making similar products (television sets). Use them to argue that small companies are preferable to large. Not all of the data is relevant.

	Up to 500 employees	Up to 1500 employees
Man-hours per set	16	23
Average wage	£120	£140
Average overtime per week	½ hr	4 hrs
Holidays	35 days	35 days
Days lost through strikes per employee	0	4
Days lost through illness or other reasons	4	11
Ratio of male: female workers	1:6	1:8
Average distance from home to work	2 kms	8 kms

3   *General knowledge – Life in the future*

Argue against either of the statements below using information from the opposing argument or from your own knowledge.

	The future will be better than today	The future will be worse than today
Population	The rate of population increase is falling. Food supplies are increasing because of new varieties and fertilisers	World population will reach 8000 million by the end of the century. The amount of cultivable land is steadily being reduced. Food supplies will not keep up with rising population.
Peace	International co-operation through the UN is improving. New communication links are drawing countries closer together.	Rivalry between big powers is getting stronger. Both sides have enough nuclear weapons to destroy the world. Six nations have nuclear bombs and at least three others are trying to make them.
Impact of technology	Machines will do the dirty, unpleasant or monotonous work. Everyone will have more time to enjoy life.	Unemployment will increase because machines can replace machine operators, clerks, librarians, shop assistants and many others. Personal privacy will disappear as computers now store many personal details about us.
Health	Life expectancy is increasing. Cures are being found for some of the major killer diseases. Smallpox has already been eradicated.	New illnesses caused by the strains of modern living will appear. Mental illnesses are increasing in the west. Diseases caused by alcohol and smoking are on the increase in the developing countries.
Pollution	Air and water pollution is decreasing in the west. New laws help limit noise pollution.	Industrial pollution is becoming serious in the developing countries. Oil pollution of the sea is getting worse. The Mediterranean is becoming a dead sea.

8 Writing about problems and solutions

To make you think

Study this illustration carefully. List all the possible dangers in this kitchen.

When you have finished, compare your list with those of other students, and together suggest ways to make the kitchen safer.

Section 1 Describing problems

Engineers, economists, planners and many others often have to examine problems and put forward the best solutions to them. The first step in this kind of writing is to state the problem clearly. Often you must say what will happen if the problem is *not* solved.

Useful language Expressing certainty

When describing consequences, you can use the following expressions to show how certain you are. The greater the number of stars * on the table, the higher the degree of certainty.

Degree of certainty	Positive	Negative
****	will, certainly	will not,
		impossible that
***	likely that	unlikely that
	probable that	improbable that
	probably	
**	may, might	may not
	possible that	might not
	possibly	
*	could	

For example, in describing the *To make you think* problem, you could write:

1 The man *will probably* trip.
2 *It is likely* that the food mixer will fall over.
3 Someone *might* be electrocuted by the kettle lead.
4 The pan of hot fat *may* catch fire.

Exercise 1
Study this car and the problems given on page 110.

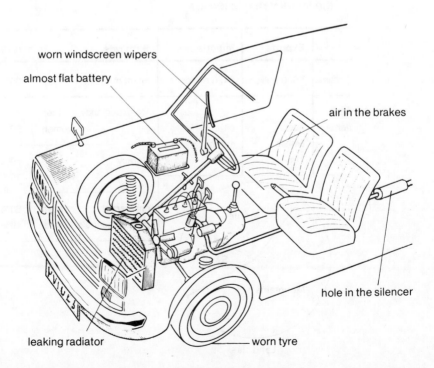

worn windscreen wipers

almost flat battery

air in the brakes

hole in the silencer

leaking radiator

worn tyre

For each fault in the car, a number of possible consequences are given. Decide about the probability of these consequences. For example:

hole in the silencer   noise, engine damage, accidents

1   It *will certainly* cause noise.
2   It is *unlikely* to lead to engine damage.
3   It *will not* cause accidents.

Problems	Possible consequences
1 *worn tyres*	skids, punctures, noise
2 *leaking radiator*	dangerous steering, engine overheating
3 *worn windscreen wipers*	vision problems in rain, serious accidents, increased petrol use
4 *air in the brakes*	tyre damage, slow braking, serious accidents
5 *almost flat battery*	starting problems, accidents, loss of speed

Exercise 2

Study this data on a developing country. Then list some of the problems of this country. For example:

the birth rate is too high
the literacy rate is too low

	Exports	Imports	Birth rate	100/1000
Totals	$350 million	$420 million	infant mortality	30%
Major items	rice timber fruit	oil defence equipment cars	life expectancy, men 48 women 52	
			literacy men 50% women 10%	
			children at boys 68% primary schools girls 18%	

Land use

Useful language   Quantity expressions: *too much, too little*

Many problems can be described in terms of *too much* or *too little* of something. The following expressions are useful. Those marked (C) can only be used with countable nouns (schools, cars, etc.) and those marked (U) only with uncountables (rice, oil, etc.)

too much (U)	*too little* (U)
an excess of	*not enough*
too many (C)	*too few* (C)
an excessive amount of	*inadequate, insufficient*
	a shortage of
	a lack of

Exercise 3
What is wrong with this diet? State the problem and describe the possible consequences of trying to live on such a diet.

Average daily intake (adult male manual worker in a tropical country)

polished rice, bread (carbohydrates)	400 grammes
oils and fats (carbohydrates)	50 grammes
meat	25 grammes
fresh fruit and vegetables	10 grammes
beans	25 grammes
milk and dairy products	0 grammes
fish	0 grammes

Notes

Deficiency in	Effect
Vitamin A (milk and butter, eggs)	blindness
Vitamin B (unpolished rice, meat, eggs)	disorders of the nervous system
Vitamin C (fruit, vegetables)	skin diseases
Vitamin D (sunlight, fish oil)	bone disease
protein (meat, fish, milk, beans)	malnutrition

Minimum levels necessary for health

carbohydrates	150 grammes
protein	70 grammes

Section 2 Presenting and comparing solutions

Exercise 4

Study this problem situation.

Fluoristan is a small, land-locked, Central Asian state. In the past its economy was based on the export of rice, animal by-products and the money sent home by those who found work in neighbouring countries. Now tourism is expanding rapidly as the magnificent
5   mountains and the unique Fluoristan temples, unfortunately in very poor repair, become better known.
Although her people are cheerful and hard-working, Fluoristan has many problems. Infant mortality is 50%. In spite of this, the population is increasing rapidly. Farming techniques are very
10   old-fashioned and food now has to be imported. Much of the land is badly-eroded hillside and semi-desert. This is due partly to cutting down forests to provide wood for heat and cooking fires. Illiteracy is above 90%. Fluoristan is a non-aligned state but has a dispute with her much bigger southern neighbour over her use for irrigation of
15   the River Danda, which forms the frontier between the two countries.
The main items in Fluoristan's Five-Year Development Plan are given below. Predict the consequences of each proposal. *Education* has been completed for you.

Ministry	Plan	Consequences
Education	Establish a university	Will bring little benefit to the country
Tourism	Build 5-star hotels	
Power	Construct a dam across the Danda to generate electricity	
Health	Sterilise all parents with more than three children	
Agriculture	Extend the Danda irrigation scheme	
Defence	Buy fighter aircraft	

When you have made your predictions, compare them with those of another student.

Useful language   *If*-sentences 1

If-sentences are used to predict the consequences of actions. For example, discussing the likely consequences of Fluoristan's Five-Year Plan, you can write:

If they *establish* a university, it *will bring* little benefit to the country.

You use the Present tense for the action and the Future for the consequence when you are discussing real proposals. Write out your predictions in the same way as the example.

Exercise 5

Make your own proposals for each of the Ministries and predict their consequences. *Education* has been completed as an example. When you have made your proposals, compare them with those of another student.

Ministry	Alternative proposals	Consequences
Education	Build more primary schools	Illiteracy reduced
Tourism		
Power		
Health		
Agriculture		
Defence		

Useful Language   *If*-sentences 2

You studied the type of *If*-sentence used to describe real proposals above. Compare this example which describes an alternative proposal.

If they *built* more primary schools, illiteracy *would* be reduced.

You use the Past tense for the action and *would* (*might, could*) for the consequence when you are describing proposals which are still under discussion and have not been agreed to. Write out your proposals in Exercise 5 in the same way.

Usually several solutions to one problem can be suggested. Each of the different solutions must be examined and the best one chosen. This is usually done by comparing and contrasting them according to effectiveness, benefits, cost, undesirable consequences, etc.

Exercise 6

Study this problem and the proposed solutions.

Hospitals in Tobania are very short of blood. People will not willingly give blood because they feel it will weaken them. In addition, there is a strong caste system and people who give blood are afraid it will go to someone of lower caste. Furthermore, about 10% of the population belong to a religion which believes that giving blood is wrong. In these circumstances, how can the hospitals in Tobania build up a blood bank?

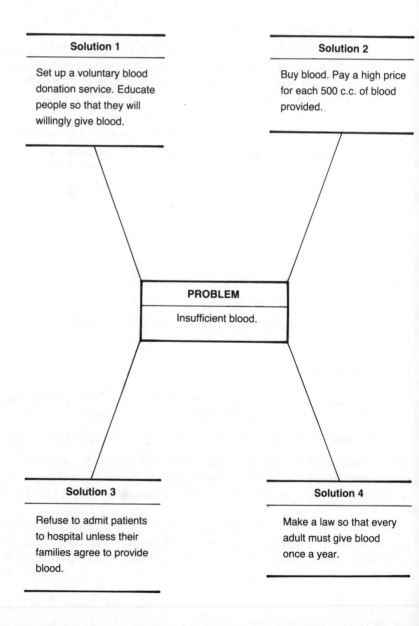

Solution 1

Set up a voluntary blood donation service. Educate people so that they will willingly give blood.

Solution 2

Buy blood. Pay a high price for each 500 c.c. of blood provided.

PROBLEM

Insufficient blood.

Solution 3

Refuse to admit patients to hospital unless their families agree to provide blood.

Solution 4

Make a law so that every adult must give blood once a year.

Now predict the consequences of adopting each of these solutions. Copy the table and write in your predictions. Add a solution of your own.

Solution	Consequence
1	
2	
3	
4	
Own	

Exercise 7
Copy and complete this table listing the good and bad points of each solution.

Solution	Good points	Bad points
1	free	will take a long time
2		
3		
4		
Own		

Using the completed table and the predictions you made in Exercise 6, write a short comparison and contrast of the proposed solutions.

Exercise 8

Study this map of Maidan and its surroundings.

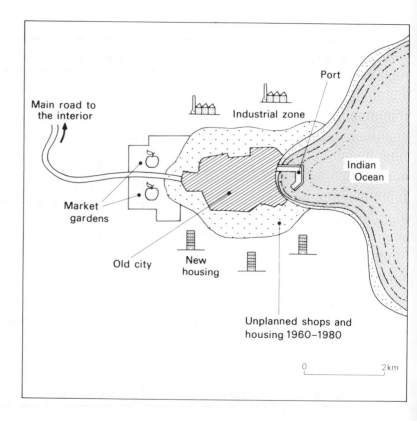

Maidan is the capital city of Manan. In the past it was a fishing port and a centre for pearl diving. However Manan has developed quickly over the past twenty years and as a result Maidan has expanded. Heavy industry has been developed to the north of the
5 city well away from the new housing in the south where many of the workers live. The port, too, has grown in size because trade has increased.

Market gardens have grown up on the west side of the city to meet the growing demand for fresh vegetables and fruit. The old centre
10 of the city remains almost unchanged. The streets are narrow and winding. The houses are old and some are in bad repair but they are typical of the old style of architecture in Manan. Unfortunately all the traffic in Maidan must pass through the old centre. Hence there are constant traffic jams.

Here are some of the possible solutions to Maidan's traffic
problems. Add three more of your own.

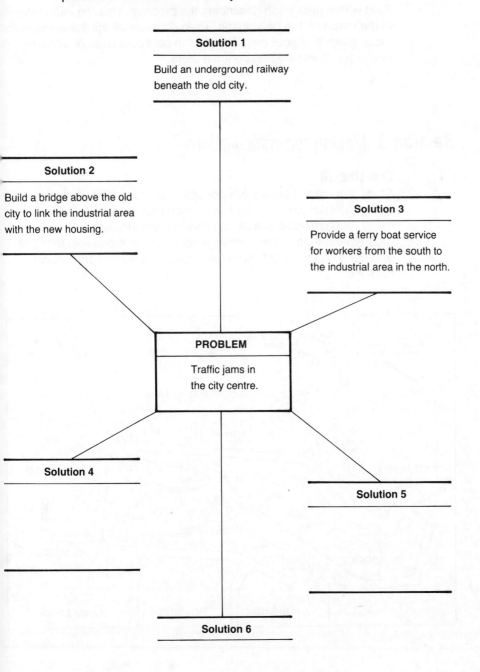

Solution 1

Build an underground railway
beneath the old city.

Solution 2

Build a bridge above the old
city to link the industrial area
with the new housing.

Solution 3

Provide a ferry boat service
for workers from the south to
the industrial area in the north.

PROBLEM

Traffic jams in
the city centre.

Solution 4

Solution 5

Solution 6

Exercise 9

Write a text about Maidan's problems and the possible solutions. Start with a paragraph describing the problem. Use the information in the map and the description. Then consider all the solutions, both those given and your own. Predict the consequences of adopting each one. Compare and contrast them.

Section 3 Making recommendations

Exercise 10

Study this map. It shows five possible sites for a cement works. Using the information in the map, recommend one site. List as many recommendations as you can to support your recommendation. Then exchange recommendations with those of another student. Decide who has provided the most convincing reasons.

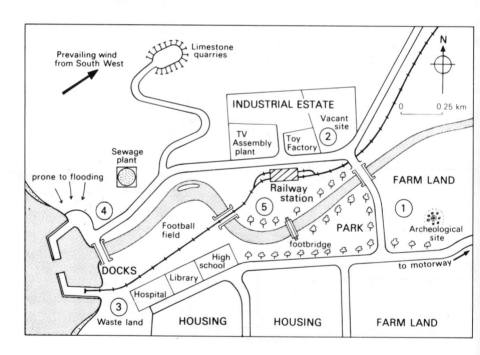

Comment

The final section in a problem and solution type of text is making a recommendation. The complete plan therefore has this structure:

Section 1   Problem stating
Section 2   Comparing and contrasting solutions
Section 3   Recommending the best solution

As with arguments, recommendations have to be supported by reasons which will convince your reader.

Useful language   Making recommendations

Study these verbs and expressions used to make recommendations in writing.

	Modal verb	be + adjective + to that	Ordinary verb
Strong recommendations	must have to	essential imperative	
Recommendations	should	advisable	advise suggest recommend

Examples:
1   The cement works *should* be built on site 1.
2   *It would be advisable to* build the works on site 2.
3   *We advise that* the works are built on site 5.

Exercise 11
Look at the map on page 118. Recommend the best sites for the following developments and give reasons for your recommendations.

1   a small factory making tents
2   a new primary school
3   a sports field for the High School

Exercise 12

Recommend a solution to each of these problems. Give reason to support your recommendation. Exchange recommendations with those of another student. He/she will reply stating whether or not your recommendation is accepted. He/she must give reasons if your recommendation is rejected.

1   The centre of the city of Zed suffers from serious traffic jams twice a day during rush hours. These occur before 8 a.m. and after 4 p.m. when all government and private offices start and finish work. There is a public bus service but only the poorest people use it. In addition, the buses often run late. Everyone else travels in his own car. As there are very few car parks, cars are parked by the side of the road. This adds to the traffic problems. There is no other form of public transport.

2   An Asian village co-operative, consisting of 28 small farms, average size 8 hectares, wants to invest in new ploughing equipment. With the money they have, they can choose from these alternatives:

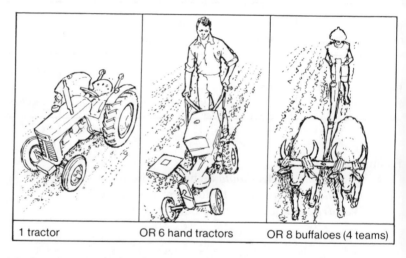

| 1 tractor | OR 6 hand tractors | OR 8 buffaloes (4 teams) |

Copy and complete this table of advantages and disadvantages.

	Tractor	Hand Tractors	Buffalo Teams
Advantages	efficient labour-saving	low fuel consumption	useful by-products
Disadvantages	expensive fuel	need maintenance	can become sick

Now write a recommendation to the head of the co-operative.

Exercise 13

Read this passage carefully, then use the information it contains to complete the diagram on the next page.

Nuclear power has often been presented as the only means of 'saving' our standard of living when the fossil fuels like oil, coal and gas run out. It is attractive in that we have already developed the technology to exploit the energy stored in the atom. In addition,
5 small amounts of fuel release enormous amounts of energy. However the problems of nuclear power have become increasingly clear in the last decade. These range from the threat of pollution to the danger of an accidental explosion and these make nuclear power a less desirable solution to the energy crisis. Furthermore, to
10 completely replace fossil fuels by nuclear power would require the construction of about fifty times the present number of nuclear power stations by the end of the century, which is beyond our resources.
   The role of alternative energy sources, such as solar energy, wave
15 power and wind power, has been researched in many countries. Studies in the USA have suggested that solar energy could provide 20% of US heating and cooling requirements by the end of the century. The same research indicates that in several countries, including Britain, wind power might be of value. Wave power
20 could also be an important source of electrical energy.
   Of these sources, solar energy in the northern hemisphere is most available when it is least needed—in the middle of the day and in summer. Moreover existing methods of energy transfer for solar power are relatively inefficient. If long-term storage could be
25 devised so that energy available in peak periods of supply could be stored for use in peak periods of demand, much greater use could be made of solar power. In contrast, wave and wind power availability match the curve of energy demand i.e. the winds are strongest and the tides are highest during the winter. For the
30 present, wind power is by far the cheapest of these alternative sources. It requires, however, aerogenerators, as big as electricity pylons, which would be sited along coastlines, where they could be very ugly.
   Using energy from the waves is still in its experimental stages. In
35 the long run, it is likely to be dearer than wind power but may still be cheaper than nuclear power.
   Some people argue that the huge coal reserves in some countries make the search for new sources of energy less urgent. But this is not facing the facts. They forget that new demands will almost
40 certainly be made on our coal reserves as a source of plastics. Coal is much too valuable to burn.

Solution 1 Nuclear power

+	−
1 The technology exists.	1 Pollution.
2	2

Solution 2 Solar power

+	−
1 Up to 20% of US heating and cooling.	1 Most available when least needed.
2	

Solution 3 Wind power

+	−
1	1 Ugly aerogenerators.
2	

Problem

Solve the energy crisis.

Solution 4 Wave power

+	−
1	1 Still experimental.

Solution 5 Coal

+	−
1 Huge reserves.	1

Exercise 14

Write an essay recommending an alternative source of power which you think particularly suitable for your own country. You may consider solutions not covered in the passage using information of your own.

Your writing should have this structure:

Section 1
The problem, its causes, and the consequence of leaving it unsolved.
Section 2
Comparison and contrast of possible solutions.
Section 3
Recommendations.

Guiding the reader   Concluding paragraphs

A concluding paragraph allows you to summarise and therefore repeat the main points in your writing. It reminds your reader of the most important points and helps you to get your message over to him.
The first step is to summarise the main points. In the passage in Exercise 13 they are:

1 nuclear power not the complete solution, possibly dangerous, too expensive
2 alternative energy sources should be considered
3 solar energy, inefficient storage
   wind, cheap but unsightly
   waves, still experimental
4 coal reserves large but too valuable

You can then link the points into a paragraph. For example:
We have shown that nuclear power is not a complete answer to the energy problem. There are problems of safety and cost. Alternative sources such as sun, wave and wind power have to be considered but, as we have seen, none is ideal. Solar power cannot be stored easily. Wind power is cheap but requires many ugly aerogenerators. Wave power is still in the experimental stages. Coal reserves are huge but, as a valuable source of raw material for plastics, coal should not be wasted.

Add a similar concluding paragraph to the essay you wrote in Exercise 14.

Section 4 Homework exercises

Select an exercise from this section which is related to your own field of study or which is of special interest to you. You can complete the exercise in your own time.

1   *General knowledge*
Study this problem.

About a third of the population of Tai Pay live on an island and two thirds on the mainland, which is two kilometres away across a stormy sea channel. Communication between island and mainland is by ferry boats but these are small, subject to delay and, in stormy weather, the trip can be dangerous.

The solutions to the problem of Tai Pay are illustrated in this diagram. Compare and contrast the solutions adding more of your own if you can. Recommend the best solution to the Government of Tai Pay.

1   *Suspension bridge*
exceptionally long span
cost $180,000,000 (Tai Pay dollars) plus
$2,000,000 a year to maintain
5 years to build,
life of 75 years

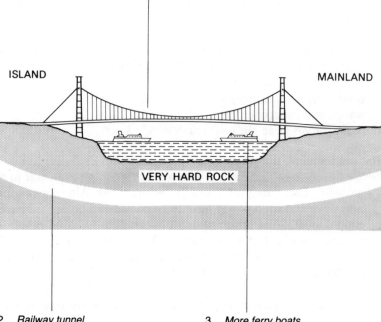

ISLAND

MAINLAND

VERY HARD ROCK

2   *Railway tunnel*
cost $250,000,000 plus $1,000,000
a year to maintain
8 years to build, life of 100 years

3   *More ferry boats*
cost $5,000,000 each
life of 15 years

2   **Medicine – The malaria cycle**
Study the diagram which shows in simplified form the malaria
cycle. Describe the cycle adding information of your own if you
wish. Then describe the solutions to the problem of malaria, i.e.
the points at which the cycle can be broken. Finally recommend
the solution you think best for a small Asian country whose
economy is based on rice production. The literacy rate is lower
than 35%.

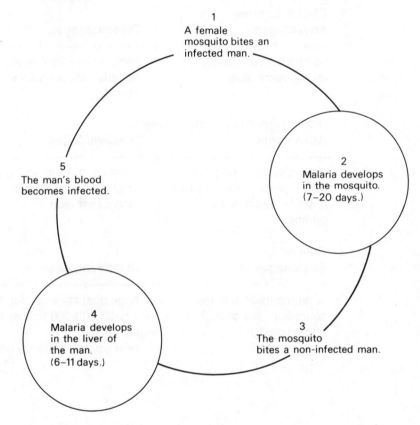

1
A female
mosquito bites an
infected man.

5
The man's blood
becomes infected.

2
Malaria develops
in the mosquito.
(7–20 days.)

4
Malaria develops
in the liver of
the man.
(6–11 days.)

3
The mosquito
bites a non-infected man.

Solutions
1   *Kill the mosquitoes*
    – drain the wet places where the eggs are laid
    – kill the adult mosquitoes with insecticide sprays

2   *Avoid contact with mosquitoes*
    fit wire mesh on windows and doors
    use mosquito nets on beds
    use insect repellent
    stay indoors at night
    keep the legs and arms covered

3   *Take drugs daily or weekly to kill the infection at the liver stage*

3   Technology – How do we transport goods and people in a world without oil?

Study these solutions. Many others are possible. Add solutions of your own. Compare and contrast the solutions, then recommend the one you think best for your country.

1   *Electric vehicles*

Advantages	Disadvantages
no pollution or noise, known technology	batteries are very heavy, batteries allow a very short range

2   *Alcohol (gasohol) powered vehicles*

Advantages	Disadvantages
Little change in engines, little change in the way fuel is sold – stations with pumps	great changes in agriculture to produce the crops from which alcohol is made

3   *Coal oil*

Advantages	Disadvantages
large reserves in some countries, little change in engine design	huge quantities of coal required e.g. 80,000,000 tonnes extra in the UK, new type of refineries needed